HOW TO MARKET THE I/S DEPARTMENT INTERNALLY

HOW TO MARKET THE I/S DEPARTMENT INTERNALLY

Gaining the Recognition and Strategic Position You Merit

L. Paul Ouellette

American Management Association

New York • Atlanta • Boston • Chicago • Kansas City • San Francisco • Washington, D.C.
Brussels • Toronto • Mexico City

Library of Congress Cataloging-in-Publication Data

Ouellette, L. Paul.
    How to market the IS department internally : gaining the
  recognition and strategic position you merit / L. Paul Ouellette.
        p.   cm.
    Includes index.
    ISBN 0-8144-5997-8
    1. Electronic data processing departments—Management.
      I. Title.
HF5548.2.085   1992
658'.05—dc20   92-2233
                                                             CIP

Printing number

10 9 8 7 6 5 4 3 2 1

Contents

Acknowledgments

It is with much gratitude that I acknowledge those who, though their names don't appear on the cover, participated directly or indirectly in the development of this book. I thank these people for their support, understanding, and ideas, which are imprinted into each page of this book.

To my wife, Elaine, who not only listened, but supported me during the challenging periods with uplifting comments and her ability to add reality to this undertaking.

To Bob Bassi of Bassi Communications, Chicago, Illinois. Bob was truly instrumental in applying his writing skills to our first draft. Bob is not only a skilled writer but also a great businessperson and friend.

To Dan Roberts, O&A President, who played multiple roles in this book from creating ideas, to rewriting paragraphs, to coordinating with all principals involved, including the publishers.

To Laurie Nicewicz, O&A Office Manager, who tirelessly took on ongoing revisions and deadlines. Her keen ability to envision the effects of the content flow of the book is very special and greatly enhanced its value.

To Mark Gould, O&A Marketing Manager, who with his knowledge of marketing coupled with his knowledge of desktop publishing worked endless hours to accomplish the completion of this book in a readable and graphic manner.

To Gerry Landry, who has taught me more about marketing through his daily behavior than anyone else I know.

To Bob Kunkle, whose writing skills put the final touches to our material.

To the following IS executives, whose input, time, and critiques were instrumental: Ken Burke, Continental Insurance; Jerry Kanter, Center for Information Management Studies, Babson

College; Dave Lombard, Bank of Ireland; Bob Parks, Public Service of New Hampshire; Diane Smigel, John Hancock Mutual Life Insurance; and George Via, Bell Atlantic.

And to our many progressive clients who have successfully adopted this book's marketing plan, techniques, and strategies into their everyday work environment to create an awareness of their value.

Illustrations

Introduction

You may well ask, "Why do I, an information processing professional (IPP), have to know anything about marketing? Especially since I've got more business than I can handle? Computer technology," you argue, "is the backbone of the corporation—they need me!"

You may be right in your thinking, and that is precisely why you will find this book enlightening, because I'll be discussing marketing and its value to you the IPP, your information systems (IS) organization, and the company that applies the skills of your profession.

For starters, let's look at some possibilities that may disclose a need for marketing. For instance, how would you reply to the following questions:

- What is the image of IS within your company?
- Do you see IS as an integral part of the overall organization?
- Are you appreciated, or undervalued?

Perhaps your pride will lead you to positive answers to all these questions. With deeper analysis, however, you may have to admit, "Yes, but . . . we're really not where we'd like to be, or should be."

This is not to blame anyone for the fact that in most American corporations IS is not considered to be foremost in the daily business thrust. Compared with other business functions, IS is still the new kid on the block, and as information processing professionals we have to remind ourselves continually about where we've been, and, even more important, think about where we're going. We may have come a long way, but still our boundaries remain unclear, and people still don't completely understand our function, how they can best utilize our services, or how they can work with us.

I started in the data processing field thirty-two years ago. It was a relatively new field at the time, exciting and on the cutting edge of the future. That's why I got into it. Well, it's still the most exciting field today. As IS professionals, we are at the front end of the power and capabilities of computerization for the corporate good, and for the way that civilization itself is being managed.

And the current recession notwithstanding, IS is still the most viable profession, offering the brightest future.

That's what this book is about. I'm going to explain why marketing yourself and your department's capability to the rest of the company is the key to your future goals and tell you how it can change the image and understanding that people have of our profession.

You may say, "I agree up to a point, but you don't know my client base. They are tough! And it's discouraging." Let me put this in perspective. I have a friend who had tough clients. He changed jobs three times. Guess what? They followed him. The moral of the story is that we feel our clients are tough because in our daily "we and they" confrontations with them we don't yet have a clear understanding of each other's responsibilities or value.

I stress this issue throughout the book. My primary objective is to help you to recognize the value you have, as well as the value marketing can have in helping your colleagues to understand your value and, especially, your technological capabilities.

I also want to explain what we refer to in our seminars as the "The Four C's to Success": confidence, competence, commitment, and consistency.

Do we perhaps give our clients an impression of being too confident and competent, perhaps a bit too smug in our knowledge of technology, while, at the same time, appearing not to be totally committed to the business and inconsistent in our assistance? And does this result in a mutual feeling that IS is not part of the business fabric? That perhaps we are, instead, a piece of lint on that fabric that could easily be brushed off! Do we sometimes not know where we stand or where we fit? Do we feel like the poor stepchild rather than a true member of the corporate family? Do we feel that our image is not what it should be? Do we have any idea of where we are going as an organization? Appropriate marketing can change all this.

When I started in the business thirty-two years ago, I'd go to parties and people would ask me what I did. I'd say that "I'm in EDP—electronic data processing," and everyone would kind of shy away. I was a guru, someone with a newfound knowledge, a star of the show.

In fact, I used to get a kick out of walking around with 5081 manila cards in my pocket, which I'd drop on the table at coffee breaks and ask if people would like me to read the holes. Yes, I was a guru and I loved every minute of it!

Now, a generation later, I say, "I'm in computers and I do some consulting," and people yawn and say, "So do I. So does he. So does she. So who cares?"

Times have changed. There's more involvement, more participation, more technology, and a lot more knowledge. Clients, whether they are internal or external to the IS organization, have become much more sophisticated in terms of our technology base. Now it's time to wrap this together and start bringing it home as a corporate value.

Charles Babbage, the English mathematician, built the first "analytical engine." Today he is generally hailed as the inventor of the computer. But in 1842, the chancellor of the exchequer asked Sir George Bidell Airy, Astronomer Royal of Great Britain, to evaluate the invention's potential. Sir George's estimate: "Worthless." As a result, the British government discontinued funding.

Such bum steers are not the exclusive property of the nineteenth century or the other side of the Atlantic. In 1943, IBM Chairman Thomas J. Watson predicted that "there is a world market for about five computers." Now if these people can make such bad calls about the marketing potential of computer technology, think how much harder it is for information processing professionals, with little or no marketing background, to convince their own organizations to buy into new technology-driven applications.

That's the main purpose of promoting the value of IS

internally: *to help IPPs create an awareness of their value and gain the recognition and strategic support they merit within their organization by the intelligent application of marketing techniques.* But before that can happen, IPPs must first convince IS and the organizations that write their paychecks. If we can create such a marketing awareness in ourselves, then we can focus on:

- Marketing and change management concepts
- Ensuring that computer solutions are driven by business needs
- Specific techniques for marketing computer technology

My hope is that this book will both reinforce what you already know, or at least suspect, and send you in new, electrifying directions. We have reached a point in IS where IPPs must think about the issues I raise, even if they don't agree with me.

Technology cannot be imposed on people and organizations. If they don't buy into our technology willingly, we may win that particular applications/technology battle but lose the bigger strategic war. And the history of organizations, as of nations, is written by the winners.

The only way to become a winner is to create an awareness of the value of your services and of the effectiveness of computer technology through effective marketing. I dedicate this book to helping you do just that: building the sophisticated human interaction and change management skills and marketing techniques essential to working effectively with your clients.

To what extent you as an IPP need to market yourself and your organization can be gauged by taking the Marketing Assessment quiz in the Appendix.

Glossary

Because I use certain words and terms in a very specific way, applicable especially to internal marketing of IS, I am providing here the definitions of such terms according to the context of this book.

client   Someone from another department within the same organization with whom the information processing professional establishes a long-term, mutually beneficial partnership based on a common desire to solve ongoing problems. A *customer*, by contrast, comes to the IPP merely to fulfill an immediate need and may never establish a working relationship. An *end user* is still further removed—a nameless, faceless entity which just happens to use the technology presented by the information systems people.

cold calling   Contacting a potential information systems client who is believed to have a problem or need for which the IS organization may have a solution. This initial contact and the ability of the IS people to create an awareness of their value sets the stage for developing a client relationship.

consultant   The information processing professional as he or she consults with peers and clients in the everyday work environment, not some high-priced guru who gets paid for advising the same thing.

demassing   The breaking down of the little empires we built across the business units when we enjoyed a technological monopoly, the little empires we created to ensure our control of technology.

EAM   Electronic accounting machine.

full-service organization   What information systems will have to be to survive successfully in the 1990s, offering their clients products, technology, service, and support that meets most of their business needs.

IPP   Information processing professional, an umbrella term that covers people in technical support functions, database administration, computer operations, application development, IS training, telecommunications, information centers, or end-user computing.

IS   Information systems, a term defining the organization of IPPs, similar but preferable to such terms as management information systems—MIS, information technology—IT (which strongly implies the technology side), or information resource management—IRM.

marketeer   One who is able to create an awareness of his or her value without hype, overpromising, or aggressive salesmanship.

MIS   Management information systems or services.

restructuring   A prominent business buzzword in the 1990s, meaning reorganization, rightsizing, downsizing, doing more with less, or flattening the hierarchy.

TAB   In the early stages of computerization, an operator who worked with tabulating equipment.

HOW TO
MARKET THE
I/S DEPARTMENT
INTERNALLY

Chapter 1

Information Systems: Evolution Becomes Revolution

All professions are conspiracies against the laity.

—George Bernard Shaw

It happened in 1982.

For the first time, computers on this planet outnumbered people. By the end of 1982, more than 5 billion computers of all sizes—from microprocessors to mainframes—were in use.

In theory, the world of IS, as found in business, should have come of age by now. That it hasn't is amazing to the casual observer who looks at how dramatically IS has changed since the introduction of electronic data processing (EDP) in the mid-1950s.

Hardware technology has improved so rapidly that what you buy today is obsolete tomorrow.

People and traditional industries have also experienced volatile change. Change has been a constant factor, and it hasn't been accidental.

In this chapter we will look at where we've been, at the road we've traveled to get where we are today. After all, the factors and situations we faced along the way account for our status and reputation at present.

But first, let me begin at the end of the evolution with the revolution that exists within the IS profession now, in the early 1990s, for it's a subject that is shaking the timbers of our hallowed halls.

It's called outsourcing, downsizing, rightsizing, or whatever word your company has come up with to describe the phenomenon of trying to be leaner and meaner in a dicey economy.

In addition, IS in the business community have evolved to a point where at times our clients are more aware of our technology and how to use it than we are. The fact that clients now consider themselves computer-literate, coupled with the fact that they can go to outside vendors for software, for hardware, and even for advice, is frightening . . . if you don't know how to promote the value of IS.

But, let me hasten to add, promoting through marketing should not be inspired by the reality of being replaced or having our services downgraded.

Sure, outsourcing is an ongoing factor facing IS today. But as you read this book, I'm sure you'll feel confident that in knowing how to market your value, you as an individual and your department will have added a new dimension to your worth to your organization.

Look at it this way, the positive way: If you're facing competition from outside sources, you are competing with a fully armed company, an organization that includes all the business disciplines, just as yours does.

It has a product to sell, and included in its presentations are the fruits of that company's collective talents. Included in this talent is a marketing organization.

You're facing this competition as a single department—a department which, until now, probably hasn't even thought about marketing.

It's too late, you say. You've already experienced outsourcing! Well, you simply have to get back in; the need for marketing is all the more intense.

You *can* compete. Never lose sight of the fact that you have the advantage—you are there—and you know your company better than any outside source could ever know it. Good IS marketing will minimize the impact. Marketing the IS value is an absolute must in the 1990s.

Figure 1-1. The four stages of information systems evolution.

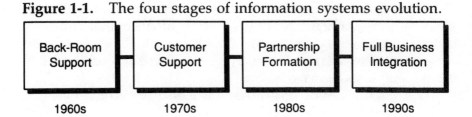

So bring on the competition! By the end of this book, you'll look on it as a challenge, not as the beginning of the end.

But if we are to understand what we must do to position ourselves for a successful future, we must study what I call the four stages of IS evolution. This evolutionary process is outlined in Figure 1-1.

Understanding the way IPPs interacted with their clients during these four stages helps us understand what has led to many of the attitudes and working relationships we have today. Many IPPs and their clients began the journey and are still interacting on a daily basis today!

Stage 1: Back-Room Support

These were the days of penciled-in totals. During the late 1950s to the mid-1960s accounting machines were totally alien "things" to most people in the corporation. This was the "better mousetrap" era of data processing (DP). The new science was viewed by management as a faster adding machine, a faster check writer, a faster filer and retriever—in short, as simply an improved way of performing accepted business functions . . . clerical functions.

That's why the world didn't exactly beat a path to DP's door. Data processing didn't look as if it were blazing new trails. The "better mousetrap" was simply moving over old ground faster. Every large corporation bought an accounting machine but not because executives were excited by the possibilities of electronic data processing. Management invested in electronic accounting machines (EAM) for the same reason it bought file cabinets. They were needed.

The reason I call this period "the days of penciled-in totals" is because, in those days, we used to run trays and trays of cards through accounting machines to come up with the final numbers. A lot of times we had card jams. Well, it was simply too inefficient to rerun all the cards so I would just pencil in the totals and say, "Trust me, it's a good total."

During this period it was basically a one-way communication (see Figure 1-2) between EDP and the client, or user, as we called them back then. But the user didn't necessarily want this output, usually didn't understand it, and, above all, didn't trust it.

A lot of our input/output was not exactly on target, it was often unreliable, and the machines frequently needed to be fixed or unjammed. The reports would be "out later."

My clients were totally dependent upon me, and I loved it. I was the TAB operator, the guru. We were a closed shop. Nobody would come onto our turf because they didn't understand the exciting high-tech world we lived in.

At the time, we proudly thought that we were dramatically accelerating the data-producing time cycle. As I look back at it now, we may actually have slowed it down in a lot of cases. Unfortunately, while doing my EAM work I didn't spend much time working on the client relationship. But time marched on.

Stage 2: Customer Support

These were the days of paper-by-the-pound. Although this narrow-focus vision reduced EDP to a glorified clerical status, that didn't stop the mid-1960s to the mid-1970s from being the era of mystique for data processing. With the high-speed 1401 system (we have 32K of memory now) and the 600 letter-per-minute high-speed printers, we could produce more Snoopy calendars faster than ever before! Technology had really arrived.

We now had our own language and titles—"autocoder" and "assembler."

I call this period "the days of paper-by-the-pound" because we produced more reports than could ever be read. We went from 6-ply to 8-ply paper and, although nobody could read the seventh or eighth copy, we didn't care. The more reports we

Figure 1-2. The simple IPP/client communications chain of the 1960s.

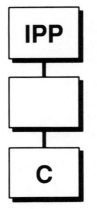

produced, the more important we were; at least, that's what we thought back then.

In fact, I remember carting dollies full of reports from department to department. I'd point to the 14-foot pile and say, "Your numbers are in here somewhere!" But time marched on.

The customer support stage continued through the mid-1970s to the mid-1980s. These were the days of sophisticated technology. Higher-speed computers allowed us to partition them off and to multiprocess! I call this period "the days of downtime" because at this time we introduced the dumb terminals, one-way communications from the computer to the client. Although we tested every element (modem, terminals, instruction sets), everything worked until we held a demonstration—then downtime! The client's favorite line was "the computer is down again!"

The computer itself was isolated behind the glass walls of its special, dust-free, temperature-controlled room. We were on display behind these glass windows. People would actually stand outside and watch this magic. Our operators used to tape signs on the windows: "Babies will be shown at two o'clock."

Oh yes, we were proud of our data center. Outside people were not admitted unless, of course, they had a badge.

At one place I worked, there was a vice-president of human resources who, like many in this compassionate function, liked to commiserate with the frontline troops. When he came to visit our data center one day, our astute, security-conscious guard stopped him and said, "I'm sorry, you can't come in without a badge, sir."

The gentlemen puffed himself erect and replied, "But you don't understand, I'm VP of Human Resources. My name is Otto Wolfe."

"I don't care if you're Peter Rabbit," our guard snapped. "No one gets in without the proper badge!"

There was still limited communication with our clients during this period. There was new technology, but our clients comprehended even less than they had before. We did improve our deliveries and they became more dependent upon us; but they still didn't trust us.

DP was quite mysterious to the uninitiated, and if the truth be known, DP folk liked it that way. Talk about an in-group! Still, in a larger sense, the in-group was really the out-group. DP was now providing the company with real benefits, but group members were no more plugged into senior management than were the people in the mailroom. Perhaps even less so. At least management knew what the mailroom did.

This is also the period when we evolved into management information systems (MIS); the client finally had two-way communications, from the terminal back to the computer, as shown in Figure 1-3. Now, although clients still lacked complete trust and understanding, they at least had screens designed for them by us and access methods they could use. A new phrase entered our language: "Trust me, it's transparent to you!"

However, we were still designing systems based on the capability of the software that was available at the time. We didn't have the flexibility we have today. Our clients had to force-fit their forms, data, access, and communications to it. But we were promoting the value of computers. We were building corporate databases; telecommunications started as a new environment of MIS. Bits and bytes were in! We started networking! We were the sophisticates with our own language. We were even bigger gurus . . . and we might have overplayed our hand.

As computer technology became more sophisticated, it became apparent that computers could do more than handle certain clerical and administrative tasks faster and more efficiently.

Figure 1-3. The more involved IPP (or MIS)/customer relationships of the 1970s.

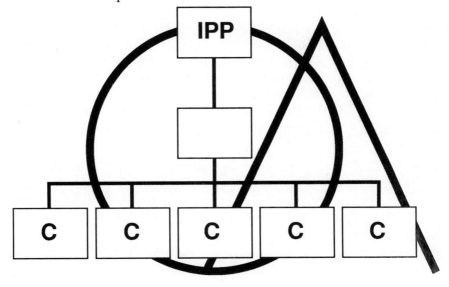

The data being processed could be shuffled around to provide management with some useful information.

Instead of just cutting payroll checks, the computer could monitor which areas of the company were incurring a lot of overtime. Instead of just cutting shipping orders, the computer could use that information to track inventory and automatically reorder at predetermined levels.

The idea that the data in the computer might be of use to other parts of the organization was the beginning of MIS as we know it today.

This elevation in status was relatively pleasant. Imagine, actually being considered a part of the business world! Because there are no free lunches, the newly dubbed MIS people also found themselves burdened with some unexpected trade-offs. These sudden burdens were called clients.

Clients were people in other departments who needed the services that MIS could provide. However, it would be unseemly to let the uninformed—whatever their rank or title—near the holy of holies, the computer. The alternative was for the MIS priesthood to leave the glass room to deal with them. It also meant that MIS now had to expand its knowledge base from such generic stuff as payroll to include some actual understanding of the specific business their employer was in. Moreover, they were still order takers, executing the policies decided upon by others, but at least they kept, and jealously guarded, their mysterious technology.

They were still the keepers of the keys, but only because no one else cared yet. That, too, would change.

Stage 3: Partnership Formation

These were "the days of user-friendly everything." Voilà! Overnight, with the introduction of personal computers in the mid-1980s, everything supposedly became user-friendly. But have you read any of your user-friendly manuals lately?

I read one the other day that referred a problem on page 14 to page 68. You guessed it! Page 68 referred me back to page 14. Imagine that, the manual was in a loop.

Seriously, the user-friendly era brought many positive signs. Clients and data processing grew closer than ever before. A link was established that encouraged two-way communication.

The friendliness of the systems made clients more knowledgeable and sophisticated. They became computer-literate. They learned how to structure a small database; how to access and/or transfer a file; how to build security measures; and how to create applications.

They became very gutsy! They started to demand service. They were even making independent decisions without help from the gurus. Departmental computing and functional computing had arrived.

Our role changed once again. We became the master keepers of the data. We were no longer owners. We were just keepers of the systems and technologies such as networking, integrated operating systems, powerful English-based languages, huge databases, systems with high reliability, and English-based emerging technology. The client had now entered our world!

The advent of minicomputers, personal computers, and workstations was the rock that technology tossed through its own glass walls. Computing came out of the computer room and into the cubicles of business. Accountants joined in running "what if" scenarios across their spreadsheets. Engineers gleefully plotted their own Gantt and PERT charts. And secretaries, hugging their word processors, tossed their last bottle of white-out into the wastebasket.

The relationship between MIS groups and their client organizations had entered a new era. No longer did clients depend upon MIS to do all the computer work for them. Instead, people throughout companies embraced the new technology as their own.

Clients now managed application design projects that depended heavily on computers. Decision making became matrix as staff, including IS, split their allegiance between their own departments and whatever interdepartmental project they were working on at the moment.

Some IS people saw this as a loss of control over their own world.

And the advent of end-user computing had ramifications far beyond the corporate walls.

I call the next phase of partnership formation the "days of the problem-solving partner." To sum up, we have actually gone from a production environment, where we were known for producing reports, to a customer environment, where we introduced computerization to our clients directly, to a partnership environment, where IS attempted to build a stronger client-IS relationship. We need to realize that in the course of this evolution we have not yet achieved the best relationship with our clients, in terms of both parties' understanding the value of the other. But for the present IS is faced with the need to understand business as never before.

The flexibility of the hardware and software now provides clients with capabilities they never previously had. Also, clients today are in direct contact with computer manufacturers and software designers, who are coming up with systems specifically designed for them, not for IS. Thus IS now has two camps to deal with—its own internal clients, and the outside vendors.

I attended a large computer manufacturer's sales meeting at which the vice-president of sales informed his sales audience, "Your new sales strategy is to go directly to the end users and tell them that with our sophisticated hardware and software they will need minimal intervention from the MIS organization."

Stage 4: Full Business Integration

The day has arrived where IS is involved throughout the corporation, from the CEO to the sanitary engineer and everywhere in between. We are an information-intense society. Our corporations operate successfully on timely information.

At this time we also need to recognize that PCs are no longer "personal computers"; they are workstations. Multi-tasking, multiprocessing, shared files, full operating systems on a micro or PC level with buffers and utilities are all realistic possibilities today. Networking at the PC level, micros with the power of minis, emerging technology such as neural systems and artificial intelligence (AI) are all coming on rapidly and recognized for all the right reasons by the client.

Technologies such as collaborative writing, voice, graphics, imaging, CAD/CAM, decision support systems (DSS), neural systems, and AI are all used or desired by the client community. We must manage these systems. We must be responsible for the migration of data from their inception all the way to their final destination. And we must make sure that the integrity issues are in place all the way through the migration path—that is, that the data remain constant and correct for all who read them.

End-user computing, application development, and databases are increasing. Chief Information Officers (CIOs) are being included in higher-level business planning within the corporation. They sit with the president's task force and decide on the use of technology for the future.

Telephone voice communications are coming into play, with IS managing that as well as data communications in a wedding of the technologies.

But our clients are now looking at technology disbursement. They see all this technology in place, but do they realize there is one area to manage it all?

Clients don't necessarily see technology management as

central. They see various separate areas of expertise, technical support, application development, end-user computing, help desk, database administration, and so forth. They generally do not link us into one department.

We need to make it known that IS is the link that connects these separate areas, through technology, for the corporate good.

In the 1970s, it was IS and the client in a one-way communication. In the 1980s, IS and end-user computing spun off to improve relationships. Some organizations have created positions such as business analyst, knowledge engineer, account manager, and others as a way of improving communication between MIS and clients. I believe this is strictly a band-aid approach to a much larger problem, but it will persist until we learn to manage and communicate directly with clients in a full business integration mode. They talked about this in the late '80s, but it's up to us to make it happen in the early '90s.

We have to start thinking about a leadership position within the corporation. We have to start managing the network effectively and we have to take the initiative in targeting business opportunities.

Our clients will continue to change. They will become even more technically self-sufficient. They will need to learn some of the systems disciplines we have learned in the past. Technology and business planning will become integrated in arriving at the overall business plan. And we must continue to stay involved and help align this technology for maximum usage throughout the corporation. The PC revolution ushered in some surprises.

The organization now needs the IS group more than ever: We are the bridge between computer technology and the in-house clients who would be using it. Corporations need IS to explain two tough questions: How can technology benefit their functions in the organization? And how will those functions adapt to the technology? IS will have to learn even more about the business of their organizations. In return, IS will have greater input into the decisions made by the organization.

This is a step up. IS has traded the priesthood for partnership. Fundamental trends are changing organizational communications for the IPP.

It used to be clear that the IPP talked directly with the client.

Today, as seen in Figure 1-4, the IPP has to work through dozens of specialty areas, as well as client functions, to get the job done. It's no longer a simple, direct one-line shot.

1990s: Full Business Integration

The best is yet to come, although that's sometimes hard to believe.

In the forty-seven years since the end of World War II, the government of Italy has been through fifty reorganizations. That's a model of stability compared to most IS groups, which seem to have surpassed Italy's record in a far shorter time span.

The constant state of flux that characterizes IS can be attributed in part to the rapid developments in technology. But this is only part of the problem. The rest is often attributable to IS senior management's falling victim to the Arbiter Syndrome: "I was to learn later in life that we tend to meet any new situation by reorganizing; and a wonderful method it can be for creating the illusion of progress while producing confusion, inefficiency and demoralization."

No, that isn't an IS manager talking about the IS group. The speaker is Petronius Arbiter, an ancient Roman author. But the problem Petronius describes, from his vantage point in the first century A.D., is still timely. Almost 2,000 years later, the Arbiter Syndrome keeps IS managers from rethinking the critical questions about the way IS functions within the corporation. For instance, should IS be centralized or decentralized? Should it be a cost center or a profit center? Should it function internally to the organization or be outsourced?

These are the general questions that we all face today, another cultural change for IS to consider in the move toward becoming a more integral part of the business community while attempting to address the most cost-effective approach to providing IS services.

Each organization has its own method of applying overhead costs, and, basically, any person or job function that is not directly involved in the development or manufacture of the product can be considered "overhead."

Figure 1-4. The complex chain of communications among IPP, specialized functions, and client in the 1990s.

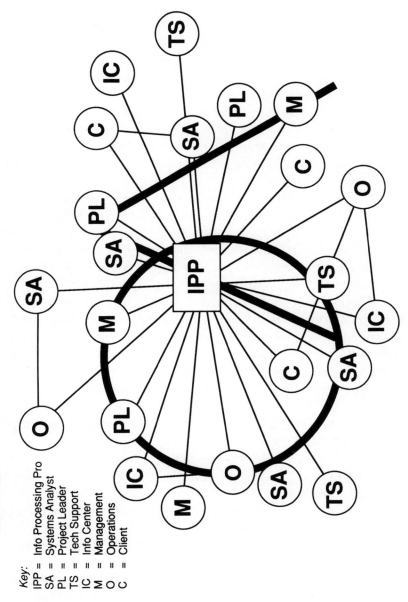

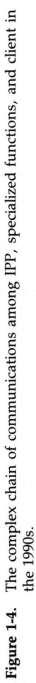

Key:
IPP = Info Processing Pro
SA = Systems Analyst
PL = Project Leader
TS = Tech Support
IC = Info Center
M = Management
O = Operations
C = Client

Although there are several methods utilized for allocating IS operational costs, in practice there have been only two theories:

1. The overhead is budgeted and actual cost is applied directly against the profit and loss statement with no attempt to charge existing profit centers.
2. The work performed is accounted for and charged back to the department requesting the work.

In either case the cost of IS is under scrutiny today as never before, and with the knowledge and hardware available, on-line, in the various departments, the swing could very well favor the decentralization of IS. The professional consequences of this trend should be obvious.

On the other hand, we cannot allow our forward progress to be impeded by the fear generated by the current focus on costs.

At this juncture, a realization of the general cost sensitivity is a must. Try to understand the methods used in your own organization so that you will be prepared to factor "cost" into your other management talents.

There are no right or wrong solutions to these problems. A solution that's perfect for one organization may self-destruct in another. Each IS organization will have to find its own answers. Nor will these be the only significant issues that IS leadership must deal with in the 1990s.

Among the hot buttons of the coming decade are:

- Continuing rapid change in both technology and corporate infrastructure
- Conflicting demands for higher productivity at lower cost
- Equally conflicting demands for higher quality but faster turnaround
- Downsizing and demassing of the systems organization
- Demands for value-added applications
- Coexistent technology complicating interface issues

Remember the days when an IS group liked to proclaim itself "an IBM house"? (Or "a DEC house"? Or any other house?) Forget it. That's history. It's already virtually impossible to stay committed to just one technology vendor. This has given rise to a new species of vendor, integration firms that mix and match technologies from different manufacturers to provide organizations with hybrid systems.

The key now is to find the right technology with the right functionality. This approach has a certain appeal to companies leery of becoming overly dependent upon any one manufacturer.

As if that's not enough, the rapid rate of technological change in the computer industry often bewilders the senior management of organizations that are utilizing this technology. Already unsure that they are getting their money's worth from the technology they already have, senior managers are increasingly reluctant to pour even more money into newer but perhaps soon-to-be-obsolete technology without a clear-cut return on investment.

The direction of these trends is clear: If IS is to remain a valued, functional part of the organization, senior management and clients must clearly know and understand the value of IS. This will lead them to make additional or different demands upon IS people—among them:

- To serve as internal consultants and to advise on the assignments of projects to specific systems
- To bring a higher level of integration to systems (even as they become more dispersed throughout the organization), a task complicated by the need to make technology more universally understood
- To fully integrate computer usage with staff needs and the business of the organization

This is of particular significance to IPPs. Our solutions tend to become our problems. The fact that a technology exists means that it will be used. The computer's ability to store vast amounts of data has encouraged an "Oh, let's enter it all" syndrome. Since what goes in inevitably comes out, organizations and the people within them are deluged by more data than they can cope with, let alone use. Even worse, this lack of selectivity confounds any sense of organizational judgment and values. We are stuck with information overload.

The ability to make creative use of computers not only to

process data but also to make sense of it is becoming noticeably more important to the long-term success and even survival of all organizations—from industrial giants to muffin shops. IS can play a leading role in extricating an organization from this lack of selectivity by redefining what it does with the data.

We must also start addressing the question of who truly owns the data: Is it the clients, executives, board of directors, or corporation? This problem is now being addressed by many corporations. Someone must be accountable for the data. I don't believe it is IS's role. To be so would require IS to focus on what science writer Ken Ringle describes as distinguishing the differences between data, information, useful knowledge, and—an old-fashioned word—wisdom:

- Data are raw facts and numbers.
- Information is what the data tell us.
- Useful knowledge is what that information means.
- Wisdom comes from applying useful knowledge to determining what strategy to follow.

The need to make such distinctions is readily apparent in what is now a trend in full bloom, the increase in the number of companies that have created the position of CIO—a chief information officer, reporting directly to the CEO. Does this mean that IS people can now sit back and bask in corporate nirvana as their organizations willingly—even gleefully—overdose on computer technology? Hardly. The long-touted Information Age arrives only when IS is accepted as a management function.

Take heart. You're almost there. IS is on the verge of ascending, to help shape management policy on the highest level. In short, fellow IPPs, you have arrived, or are at least within sight of land. This leaves only one question to be answered: How can we IS people help our clients to better understand us so that they can make more efficient use of our technology and services? The next two chapters are devoted to answering this question.

Chapter 2

Human Barriers to Change

To: President Andrew Jackson,

The canal system of this country is being threatened by the spread of a new form of transportation known as "railroads." The federal government must preserve the canals for the following reasons: One. If canal boats are supplanted by "railroads" serious unemployment will result. Captains, cooks, drivers, hostlers, repairmen and lock tenders will be left without means of livelihood, not to mention the numerous farmers now employed in growing hay for horses.

Two. Boat builders would suffer and tow-line, whip and harness makers would be left destitute.

Three. Canal boats are absolutely essential to the defence of the United States. In the event of the expected trouble with England, the Erie Canal would be the only means by which we could ever move the supplies so vital to waging modern war.

For the above-mentioned reasons the government should create an Interstate Commerce Commission to protect the American people from the evils of "railroads" and to preserve the canals for posterity.

As you may well know, Mr. President, "railroad" carriages are pulled at the enormous speed of 15 miles per hour by "engines" which, in addition to endangering life and limb of passengers, roar and snort their way through the countryside, setting fire to crops, scaring the livestock and frightening women and children. The Almighty certainly never intended that people should travel at such breakneck speed.

> Martin Van Buren
> Governor of New York
> January 31, 1829

Today this letter by the soon-to-be President of the United States seems laughable; 163 years ago it was dead serious. Mr. Van Buren's "facts" and insight into the intent of the Almighty are as outdated as the canals he sought to protect. However, the emotion that prompted the letter is as timely for IPPs as neural systems.

Consider the case of Charles H. Duell, who urged the President of the United States to abolish the U.S. Office of Patents on the grounds that "Everything that can be invented has been invented." What makes this statement so curious is that Mr. Duell offered this argument in 1899, when he was commissioner of the agency he proposed closing.

Duell is perhaps guilty only of a lack of imagination. He is the sort of person who narrows the concept of the possible to fit the confines of his or her own little views. Such people usually consider their opinions to be immutable laws of the universe. Van Buren, on the other hand, is a more serious case. He provides us with insight into one of the most basic human motivations— fear of change.

I'm not talking about cyberphobia—fear of computers—here. I'm talking about any kind of change. To prepare ourselves for the new, we must accept change. It's amazing to me, but I must confess that during my thirty-two years working throughout the IS ranks, I have found IPPs most reluctant to change. Now take it easy, I know this doesn't happen in your organization, but in others. . . .

Preparing the IS organization for change may be the most important function of management today. This brings us back to old-fashioned words such as *values* and *ethics*.

Why should we bother ourselves with values and ethics in a book on marketing the value of IS internally? Because values and ethics, I feel, often correlate with background and environmental circumstances, and are the way we look at the world. Values determine needs. Needs determine goals. Ethics determine how we approach our goals. And together, values, needs, and ethics determine the function and future of our organizations. Trying to market while ignoring them is like working without a total environmental understanding. You just might lose something.

No organization can be successful without planning. Yet corporate planners often have great difficulty in planning properly. Why? Because most planning assumes a neutral, passive environment? Wrong. Human nature dictates at least passive resistance and, more likely, active resistance to just about any change. This includes resistance to doing what's necessary to make something happen, even when those resisting are aware of the need to make it happen.

Before an organization attains a high degree of unanimity of opinion, there are different levels of negative "attitude" that the IS marketer must deal with so as to make his or her real value understood:

- *Apathy*. They know but they just don't care. They don't even care about apathy.
- *Uncertainty*. They aren't really sure.
- *Misunderstanding*. They are sure, but wrong.
- *Ignorance*. They simply don't know.
- *Lack of awareness*. They don't even know that they don't know.
- *Dissatisfaction*. They're rejecting you on the basis of prior experience.
- *Fear*. They're afraid on the basis of what they know.
- *Lack of confidence*. They may trust your motives but not your competence. (The late Owen D. Young, a lawyer, industrialist, and statesman, when chairman of General Electric, sounded the alarm on this one: "It is not the crook in modern business that we fear, but the honest man who does not know what he is doing."
- *Distrust*. They don't trust the corporation, IS, technology, or any combination thereof.
- *Hostility*. They are openly antagonistic.

This isn't abstract theory. It's the real-life example of the unemployed but highly intelligent administrative assistant who took two years to find another job because her fear of computers kept her from ever learning even basic word processing ("I could never learn that stuff"). It's the department head who's been keeping a duplicate set of manual records for eleven years "just in case."

You know the type. But rather than fight them, let's try to

understand them by bringing some perceptiveness to human foibles.

Consider that each of us is an onion; each layer represents something we believe. To some extent, these layers of belief can be peeled away from us.

The outer layers are thin, superficial, and easy to remove. They consist of stuff like what brand of toothpaste or toilet tissue we prefer. There's no big deal making a change here. No one's going to go berserk if she finds a different brand of toothpaste on the bathroom sink. If she does, you're out of psychographics and into psychoceramics, the study of crackpots.

As you go a little deeper into the onion, however, getting someone to change becomes somewhat tougher:

"I'd much rather have a dog than a cat" (or vice versa).
"Apple? This is an IBM shop!" (or vice versa, or substitute your own brand names).

As you penetrate to the center of the human personality, you reach the core. There each of us holds our most cherished beliefs, the ones we'll go to the wall for. For most people, these include, but are not limited to, religion, close relationships, politics, patriotism, and other matters of principle that are of great moment to us (although one person's middle-onion opinion may be someone else's core belief).

The closer you get to their core beliefs, the more difficult it is to influence people. These beliefs are easy to reinforce and tough to negate. Why?

Homeostasis. That's the basic activity of the human race and can be described as keeping our little world just the way it is. Perverse though it may seem, we would rather have the imperfect world we know than the more perfect world we could reach by taking action. Homeostasis helps explain the inexplicable—from the serious (battered wives who won't leave their husbands) to the whimsical (fans who remain loyal to the Boston Red Sox with a determination that defies all understanding).

This resistance to change is true of our physical environment. When was the last time you moved to a different house or apartment just because you thought moving was fun? It's even more true of our psychological world. You threaten my security, and I'll fight you tooth and nail.

That's hardly an overstatement. Take a modest example. One corporate public relations department was dragged into the computer age by an IS organization that equipped its members with PCs and the word processing package that was company issue at the time. This particular software was about as user-friendly as a 55-pound backpack. Of course, the PR department complained about the PCs for two weeks and about the software for two weeks after that. But by that point they were in love with word processing. The software package was still awful.

IS found a better system that was more flexible, much easier to use, and had more features. But they were never able to persuade most of the PR department to try it. Why? Because the old software, awful as it was, was by now as familiar as an old pair of comfortable shoes. Why get corns breaking in a new pair?

The people in the PR department were hired because of their creative ability. This was clearly demonstrated in some of the reasons they came up with for not changing over to the new software: "The manual clashes with my office decor." "I'll wait for the movie version." "I don't fondle foreign floppies." The real reason: homeostasis, of course.

To defend the status quo, our minds resort to cognitive dissonance, which is the clinical term for the bad vibes we get from something new. In fact, we go to great lengths to ignore information that disturbs our mind-set:

- *Selective exposure.* That's the first line of defense. People only accept new information that reinforces their beliefs. Or, as our mothers used to tell us, "You only hear what you want to hear."

- *Selective perception.* The second line of defense is our message filter. It's how we deal with information that contradicts our beliefs. Simple. We just twist it around until it fits our view. It's like the story about the nineteenth-century farmer who went to a carnival where he saw his first elephant. He looked at it, touched it, and then turned away, saying, "There's no such animal."

- *Selective retention.* If all else fails and stuff we don't like gets through anyway, there's no problem. We simply edit our memories until the experience comes out the way our world would want it. This is the cause of nostalgia for the good old days, which never existed. The human mind is a wonderful thing. It selectively un-remembers those parts of the past that were crummy.

All this to avoid change. It's like being part of a trapeze act. The worst part is that brief interval between letting go of one trapeze bar and catching the one on the other side. It's only a matter of seconds. But for that instant, you've given up the comfort of what you had to move toward something you don't have and don't know. That can be scary. "Better the devil I know than the devil I don't" is an all-too-normal human reaction.

Because IS people have been known to raise the occasional teeny objection—rare occurrence, of course—you may now be asking this question: "If it's that tough to get anyone to change anything, how come we're not still living in caves?"

Because of anomalies. These are the occasional jarring facts that get through our defenses. One is no big deal—just a blip on the mental radar screen. Two or three? No problem—just a few bugs in our psychic software. But what if these blips keep punching holes in our defenses? What if the blips keep piling up until we can no longer ignore them? That's when change happens. That's when the devil we don't know becomes preferable to the devil we do.

When enough people make that leap, it becomes a trend. This is not something that happens overnight. It's a very rare event that can change everyone's opinion instantaneously. In my consulting business, we have several progressive IS client organizations committed to changing their culture. I'm talking about moving several hundred people to what I call the "New Wave IS" environment, and about them making a two-, three-, and up to five-year commitment to this change process.

Generally, acceptance is distributed over a five-phase process called the innovation curve, illustrated in Figure 2-1. It quantifies the diffusion of innovation, telling us what everything from men wearing earrings to protesters against the Vietnam War must achieve to win overall acceptance.

Figure 2-1. The innovation curve for acceptance of new ideas.

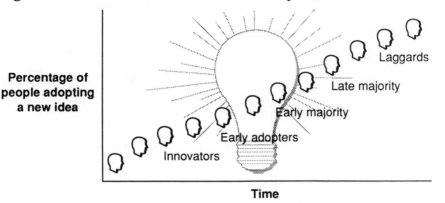

These are the five types who make up the curve:

1. *The innovators.* These are the first to accept any new concept, idea, or trend. At the extreme end of the innovators are the trendies who will do anything just to be different. (The homeostasis of trendies is based on change. They are the people who actually ran out and bought Nehru jackets.)

2. *The early adopters.* This 20 to 25 percent are the front-line troops of the majority. When they move toward an idea, it's the first sign of eventual broad-scale acceptance.

3. *The early majority.* With this 20 to 30 percent coming in, the trend is nearly irreversible.

4. *The late majority.* This last big chunk (20 to 30 percent) pretty much means total acceptance for the innovation.

5. *The laggards.* This final 10 to 20 percent are the mirror opposite of the innovators. Laggards are last to accept anything. Some of them never do. At the extreme end of the laggards are the people who still believe that the world is flat.

Before you, in IS, can get someone in the organization to make a change, make sure that you know where that person falls on the innovation curve. If you decide on a pilot program, make sure you choose a department with some innovators—not one staffed with laggards.

In planning for change, you must also consider the six basic steps that anyone—innovator, laggard, or in between—must go through before they accept something new:

1. *Awareness*. First, you have to know it's out there. It's virtually impossible to buy a computer if you've never heard of such a gizmo.
2. *Interest*. What's in it for me? What are its features and benefits?
3. *Trial*. This is where you take a risk. It may be minimal, like trying a free sample of LOTUS. Or the risk could be significant, like going to a different manufacturer of mainframes.
4. *Decision*. This is sink-or-swim time. You are ready to make a commitment.
5. *Action*. It's a done deal.
6. *Reinforcement*. Now you ask yourself: Did I do the right thing? Here homeostasis is your friend. Your mind-set gladly accepts anything you can come up with that makes the decision seem a good one.

Before you try to get your organization or any part of it to accept an innovation, you better pinpoint how far along they are in this process and match your arguments accordingly. Don't try to force a trial until your clients are clear on how the new application might benefit them.

To the IS mind, all of this may seem to be "soft," "touchy-feely" stuff that is impractical and hard to quantify. And at first it does raise more questions than it answers. But as James Thurber pointed out, "It is better to know some of the questions than all of the answers." (From John Bartlett, *Bartlett's Familiar Quotations*, Boston: Little, Brown and Company, 1980)

Like it or not, marketing change, and being successful at it, requires dealing with the most powerful, ultimate software of all, the human mind.

Chapter 3

Why IS Is Not Well Understood

We have met the enemy and they is us.

—A remark by Pogo in the Walt Kelley comic strip

In my travels and in my work with the many IS organizations across the breadth of the United States and overseas, I get a clear message that IS is misunderstood! Forget for a moment who's a good guy or a bad guy, the us and them. IS is simply not understood as an organization. People see pockets of expertise, technical support, application development, and end-user computing, but they do not view us as one unit.

Why has IS come to be understood so segmentally? The answers—and there are more than one—have to do with both the nature of IS as a profession and the nature of the people attracted to it.

What Business Are You in?

In the spirit of equal opportunity, this one's for the IS organization. At your next IS staff meeting, bring in a stack of blank 3×5 file cards. Give each person one card. Ask the information processing professionals to take pen in hand and write on the card the answer to one simple question: "What business are you in?"

This shouldn't take more than 30 seconds unless they're translating their answers into binary code. Now go around the table and ask each person to read his or her answer.

Unless your IPP group is highly unusual, you will probably get such answers as "systems," "data processing," "computer applications," and the names of some of the areas of specialization within your discipline ("programmer," "analyst," "technician").

These are all perfectly reasonable answers. But they are not acceptable. The IPPs should have provided answers more in line with their clients' line of business, such as "banking," "plumbing supplies," or whatever it is that the company does to sustain operational life. Because IPPs tend to identify more with their profession than with their client's business, their clients find it difficult to relate to IS as an integral part of the organization's business.

Clients view IPPs not only as outsiders but as outsiders with the ability to stand alone—the "don't call us, we'll call you" syndrome.

The greatest single failing of the computer industry as a whole is its refusal to adapt to end users. We tend to be pure technicians and are generally known by the client community as installers of technology rather than as implementors of technology. We hear of a need from our clients, find a technical solution, install the technology, test it, leave a few instructions and perhaps a manual behind, and tell the client, "Go for it!" Our measurement of success seems to be: "We are not receiving any problem calls; it must be working." Here are just two examples of our aloofness:

1. *A refusal by a majority of IPPs to speak in English.* We use tech-speak, the inflated professional and technical jargon that obfuscates more than it clarifies. Consider the IPP who told a new client to "deactivate the PC's energy input and then attempt a hard reboot of the system." Really . . . wouldn't it be easier—and a lot more human—to say "turn it off and start over"?

2. *A refusal to provide manuals that are comprehensible to clients.* Perhaps somewhere out there is a piece of hardware or software that a client could install simply by following the instructions in the manual. But I doubt it.

Computer illiteracy, though changing fast, is still a fact of life for many clients that should be kept in mind.

The Paperless Office and Other Pies in the Sky

This criticism should not give the impression that IPPs are incompetent. Far from it. Typically, IPPs are well-qualified professionals who know what their systems can do. But at times they ignore the most treacherous software—people.

This refusal to consider the human factor is the source of another organizational black mark against IPPs. Additionally we carry a reputation for our projections often being wrong.

Remember the promise of the paperless office? The one that was supposed to arrive by the mid-1980s? Why didn't this paperless utopia come about, thereby saving a couple of zillion trees? It didn't happen because the futuristic technical projections were too optimistic. They were based solely on what the technology was capable of, but did not consider people's desire, willingness, or ability to absorb the technology. Projections such as this assume that people will want all these microchip goodies. The reality is something quite different.

Forecasting is tough under the best of circumstances. It's too easy to fall into the trap of projecting on the basis of false assumptions. One study of emerging technologies showed that 53 percent of the forecasts that failed were based on false assumptions, unrestrained optimism, and a market that wasn't there. The other 47 percent of the forecasts were on target because of the preexistence of market factors that reinforced the need or desire for the technology.

Too often IPPs have extended the reach of the IS organization only to find that business doesn't want it. Because IS is viewed at times as pushing technology for which there is no apparent payback, senior management may see IS as a source of million-dollar solutions for hundred-buck problems: a cost center without results, a high-tech hole in which management is asked to pour increasingly large amounts of money.

If business can be said to have a religion, it would be the worship of numbers. When management looks at IS, it weighs the IS organization in terms of the bottom line. That's why it is convinced that business results and technological results/ measurement are foreign to its IS operation.

Technological innovation means more than coming up with new capabilities. It must add value. Technological utilization must be task-driven. When your clients have a real business need to use your technology—and use it themselves—to do their jobs, you will have converts. Otherwise, it's like the work of art—a machine of sorts—on exhibit in a glass case at New York's LaGuardia Airport. The case is filled with wheels, ramps, and an amazing assemblage of metal, matter, and other varieties of junk—plus large ball bearings that whiz up, down, around, and through the mechanism with abandon.

This Rube Goldberg contrivance is like technology mad-capped by the Marx Brothers. It's expensive and fun to watch but accomplishes absolutely nothing. And that's exactly how your technology will be viewed unless it plugs into what's really happening in your client's business.

The Real Revolution

The shift to an information-based service economy is the real revolution. The technology is just the tool that makes it possible. That's why the "computer revolution," as far as it's already come, still has a long, long way to go before it's complete.

Have you ever seen a kid kick an anthill just to watch the ants scurry around in a state of complete agitation? That's as good an analogy as any for the impact of new technology on the employees of an organization. Technology changes people's objectives. It changes their organizational relationships—drasti-cally and often. It even changes the jobs of those at the bottom of the corporate pyramid. And the way these technology changes come about is, to some people, insidious.

Most technologies are introduced as one-to-one substitutions for existing technologies. But new technology almost always has other capabilities. After taking care of the boring stuff like payroll and inventory, data processing began to understand the other possibilities of computers. While still doing the donkey work, computers began to expand their scope to the more sophisticated, fun stuff. That's when people really started to worry.

For example, many IS organizations are surprised to find that sales departments resist the introduction of voice mail. This is a more efficient way of converting information, but the sales reps may see it as interfering with customer relationships. It's also why customers—or would-be customers—often hang up when they phone a company and hear, "To reach customer service, press 1. To reach. . . ." The customer often perceives the electronic intermediary as dehumanizing, as an impersonal interference with the caller's relationship with the company. The customer has a point. Organizations are built not on information but on relationships. The information is important, but it's only a by-product.

Information and the Financial Markets

For another example of expanding technology, look at the financial markets. Trading in stocks and bonds, options, and futures traditionally has taken place in trading pits on the floors of the nation's exchanges. These are not restrained, gentlemanly affairs. In fact, many resemble rematches of professional football's bitterest rivals. Yet even the most chaotic trading crowds—which can number up to 400 traders, all screaming and waving for each other's attention—are focused on computer screens bringing in real-time information: stock and commodity prices, corporate announcements, news of droughts and dividends, war and peace.

The introduction of computers in the nation's stock exchanges meant faster order flow, real-time prices, and better order executions. Yet the same technology has also created pressure for computerized, off-floor trading. The logical outcome of such a development would be the demise of the exchange's trading floors. (It's already happened in London.) While there are many valid arguments on both sides of this issue, what do the exchanges, their traders, brokerage firms, investors, and government regulators believe is the impact of this technology?

Shaking Up the Pyramid

Any major organizational change—and that's what new technology often means—initiates a realignment of power, status, and resources. Some gain, others lose.

We need to understand the full implications of computer technology. Your technology is lobbing grenades at the organizational pyramid. Your computers affect everyone's job—from the CEO's to the sanitary engineer's. The people at the bottom of the pyramid fear that they will be computerized out of a job. Equally fearful—and with good reason—are first-line supervisors and middle managers. An automated work force needs less supervision. The ranks of the next level up are also being chopped back by computers, which are usurping middle management's traditional role as passers and processors of information.

You are the innovator, the agent of change. But unfortunately, all too often, you are burdened with the image of a change tyrant, the person who rams innovation down the organization's throat with no regard for the human cost.

Into another department you walk, clipboard in hand and that technological gleam in your eye, telling clients, "trust me." The employees you are blithely telling this to have lived through an era that stretches from Watergate to Irangate, from Vietnam to the current S&L bailout fiasco.

These experiences have taught people one simple lesson: Anytime that someone in a position of authority says, "trust me," immediately hide your loved ones, bar the door, count your fillings and fingers, clutch your wallet or purse and sit on it. Because to John and Jane Q. Public, "trust me" means they are about to get stiffed.

As manager of change, you have a lot to overcome. Knowledge of the business and sensitivity toward the role of others is a good place to start.

Up to this point we have reached an understanding of the mixed messages we convey to our clients. Knowing this helps us to understand why marketing the value of IS may be necessary. We now look more directly at what marketing is.

Chapter 4

What Is Marketing, Really?

Marketing is creating an awareness of your value.

—*L. Paul Ouellette*

Remember Clark's Third Law? "Any sufficiently advanced technology is indistinguishable from magic." For the average IS client, what could be less real than the thought of electrons racing around like little lab rats inside a plastic box, through a series of infinitesimally small open or closed switches, just to tell us if we have misspelled a word? That's unreal.

What is real is your need to market IS to your organization. Before you can accept that statement at face value, it might be helpful first to clear up some misconceptions about marketing.

What Marketing Is Not

Marketing is not hype. Admittedly, hype is often found in marketing campaigns. But hype is a sign that someone is trying to artificially inflate either a bad marketing campaign or a bad product or service. The best marketing is built on honesty and sincerity.

Marketing is not selling. Lots of people make this mistake (including some people in marketing). If, for example, I say "big apple," you may well respond "New York City." Through effective marketing, the label "big apple" brings New York City to mind, but no one is selling you the city. Selling is very concrete. It's the delivery of "something"—a product or service—in exchange for money or its equivalent.

Successful selling is straightforward and easy to measure: The client signs on the dotted line. The buyer buys something, the seller sells. Both roles are clear. Assessing successful marketing and, in this case, successful marketing of your IS organization is less clear-cut.

The Real Thing

Marketing is a matching process by which a producer provides the right mix of four variables:

1. Product or service (function and features)
2. Price (terms and conditions)
3. Promotion (advertising, public relations, and other marketing communications to build awareness and understanding)
4. Distribution (availability and convenience)

These variables do not exist in a vacuum. All four must be combined in a way that meets the client's need.

Marketing has never sold a single product or service. That's the sales rep's job. Instead, think back to our discussion of the six steps necessary before people accept something new: awareness, interest, trial, decision, action, and reinforcement.

Good marketing is a process whose primary goals are to raise awareness and interest—in short, consciousness. The object of marketing is not to get clients but rather to educate them, to get their commitment to support our organization and technology.

For the IPP, the goal of marketing IS internally is to give clients a general understanding and appreciation of what IS is all about—how it can be utilized as a partner to help meet business goals.

In this sense, one can draw a parallel between the marketer and the systems analyst (although I'll again state that all IPPs need to be marketing every day). The analyst acts as the middleman between the client, on the one hand, and the programmers and other IS people who will meet the client's needs, on the other. In the same way, the marketer studies the client's needs in order to make the best recommendation to the supplier of the product or service. In each case, the result is an investigation aimed at producing the best possible solution for the client.

The Mark of Good Marketing

The analogy between systems analysis and marketing can be extended a little further. Just as slipshod systems analysis results in systems failures, cost overruns, and half-baked "solutions," sloppy marketing guarantees a product without a market or clients without the products they really need or want. Marketing kludges are about as useful as computer kludges.

To be effective, good marketing should be:

- *Dynamic*. The IS marketing program should be undergoing a constant reassessment of client needs.

- *A long-term process*. Marketing is not a one-shot deal. There are no quick fixes. Band-aid marketing doesn't work.

- *Focused on new opportunities*. The best way to improve the status of IS is to search out the organization's needs and problems and provide solutions for them. Take a problem off someone's desk and make it go away and you will have a friend for life. Or at least through the next budget cycle.

- *Qualitative*. One of the most basic premises of marketing is: "Truth is a ceiling above which marketing cannot rise." If you've got it, flaunt it. But if you flaunt it, you darn well better have it. Good marketing cannot help a lousy product or service. In fact, if a product or service is really bad, a great marketing campaign just speeds up the process of sending the product or service off the cliff. The marketing campaign helps people to become aware of the product or service—and its failings—that much faster. Remember "New Coke"?

Indicators of How You Are Doing as a Marketeer

How do you know when you are marketing your IS organization successfully and effectively? There are clear-cut indicators of both good and bad marketing of technology.

Let me start with a couple of true stories, based on my own personal experience, on how not to market yourself or your organization:

THE "CORK TRICK"

I was a featured speaker during a very prestigious conference held at one of the country's storybook resorts for managers of a major American corporation. I was elated at the audience's reaction to my program, and, as we discussed how to be consultants and marketeers, I was frankly overwhelmed by their enthusiasm.

My wife and I were invited to the dinner that concluded the conference. People came to our table during the dinner and commented on the success of my presentation, and in the spirit of the evening I innocently introduced a parlor trick to those at our table. My "cork trick" is a bit of a legerdemain involving two wine corks, a simple but fascinating transfer of corks from one hand to the other.

In no time at all the cork trick spread to all the tables; people were even getting extra corks from the bar in order to try it. I was the hit of the evening! The life of the party! A huge success, right?

Wrong!

It seems that the manager responsible for the entire conference, the number two man in the IS organization at the time, was not amused. He had hired a band and all, and felt strongly that my cork trick detracted from the mood he had hoped to generate—and he told me so, in no uncertain terms! I apologized. But, as you may have guessed, shortly thereafter this gentleman became number one—and his door is now closed to me.

THE "END RUN"

We had been working with a large company for three years and had always been given to understand that the Ouellette & Associates' programs were the best this company's employees had attended.

To clarify, let me say that I reported to Executive A. I was a keynote speaker at one of the firm's managerial conferences and there met Executive B, who was the top executive. In my discussion with B, I told him more about O&A and asked if I could meet with him to see if there was more we could do for his company. He agreed and asked me to call his secretary; and I did.

There was also Executive C, a high-level manager whom I had met—in fact he had introduced me when I was the keynote speaker— but with whom I'd had no other contact.

When the date for my appointment with Executive B approached, I called my regular contact, Executive A, and was told that he had been replaced by Executive C.

Well, the appointment was with Executive B after all, and since I didn't know Executive C that well, I went ahead with my meeting with Executive B without notifying C.

Once again, you've guessed it.

Executive C was livid and called me the next day to make sure I knew he was. To think that I had met his boss without notifying him! I wrote a letter of apology, but to no avail. Our business with that client stopped. His door is also shut!

The moral of these stories is that the marketeer must be extremely sensitive to organizational structures, and especially to the human personalities within that environment. I cannot stress this enough.

In the case of the cork trick, I had stolen the show from the program director with my simple diversion. From my mistake I hope you'll learn that the marketeer's role is to listen: *Never take the play away from the client.*

In the case of the end run, although I could justify keeping my appointment with Executive B, I had overlooked the sensitivity of Executive C.

Both cases are examples of innocent actions that had disastrous results. We must constantly be aware of the political climate within an organization. We must keep attuned to the players and, above all, listen. What is a joke to you could seem like an insult to someone else. Such is corporate America!

Do you know how well you are marketing yourself? Well, let me ask you a question: Were you invited to participate in next year's budget plan and/or budget meetings? You're in the minority of IPPs if you answer yes to this question. Very few of us are invited, but we should be!

The point is that awareness of our role and of our capabilities is still not where it should be, so, obviously, we need to concentrate on marketing.

Positive Indicators Suggesting Good Marketing

- People from your corporate business community request that your IS group be more involved in their business. They want you to help them put their business plans and strategies together and to review and influence their technology decisions.

- Your budget requests are met without your constantly having to justify your existence and defend your contributions to the organization.

- Your current clients refer others within the organization to you.

- Requests for your assistance are becoming more focused, that is, more in line with the products and services you actually provide.

- You are receiving unsolicited positive feedback from your clients and senior management.

- You are asked to participate in higher-level strategic planning for your company.

Negative Indicators, Suggesting a Strong Need for Marketing

- There is uncontrolled, random purchasing of technology throughout the corporation. When everyone "does their own thing," technologically speaking, guess who'll be blamed for incompatibility problems? ("Systems shoulda told us . . .").

- You get complaints from clients that things are taking longer than planned, that commitments are not being met. One

IS group, with a critical, major system under development, was so far behind schedule that the rest of the corporation grimly referred to IS as the Bermuda Triangle. Projects went in, but never seemed to come back out.

- You hear repetitious questions concerning why your group exists and what you actually do.

- You are constantly targeted for budget cuts.

Even if your IS group has not fallen prey to these negative indicators, there's one fact that I cannot emphasize too strongly: Marketing your IS organization is like doing housework—you're never really done. Stop cleaning and the house gets dirty. Stop marketing and you lose touch with your client community.

Creating an Awareness of Your Value

IPPs are generally more comfortable with the concept of marketing when they focus on its educational aspect. Success in this educational effort will, of course, benefit the IS organization. That's why I define marketing as creating an awareness of your value.

"Wonderful!" says the unconvinced IPP. "Just what I need: one more thing to do." That attitude is understandable. The typical IPP is overbooked and overburdened with projects. The word *marketing* conjures up visions of more projects, more clients, more headaches. "Terrific!" the lament continues. "With all the roles I already play in this organization, you're telling me I now have to be a marketer? I have to market my organization?"

In the immortal words of Gary Cooper, "Yup." In fact, a resounding "yup."

In the first place, the same is true of your clients. They, too, have a lot to do and are asking if they have to take their valuable time to learn and implement your systems. The answer to the client side of this question is still "yup."

They need your products and services to do their jobs better, and you do have to market the technology to them if you and your group want to fulfill your roles successfully and effectively.

There's a ton of hardware and software out there. It's been estimated that there are more than 30,000 different software packages now available in the United States, with a new idea coming out of Silicon Valley—or someone's basement—every 30 seconds.

Some of your clients think they need it all. Some don't want any of it. Without a well-conceived marketing strategy for implementing technology, you and your company could become victims of overload, confusion, or replacement.

Marketing can mean the difference between an IS organization that is merely an administrative function or back-room support service and one that plays an influential, strategic role in the organization, with an influential impact upon client business plans.

By creating an awareness of your value through effectively marketing the IS organization, you allow IS to gain the recognition and strategic position within the corporation it deserves. Marketing can position the IS organization for high-payoff opportunities and the more desirable projects that have a significant impact on the business goals of the corporation—the bottom line.

Marketing should be thought of as the best way to position the IS organization for the future. It is not simply a way to get more business and increase overload. Marketing is the way to get the right opportunities that will brighten the future of the IS organization. It was in this larger context that Peter F. Drucker argued that "business has only two functions—marketing and innovation." (From *Money Talks*, New York: Facts on File, 1985)

IS should be the crossroads where these two functions meet. Technical innovation without the marketing necessary to convince the corporation of the need for it is only half the equation. And no one can successfully solve half an equation. Consider the cosmetic company research department that developed a hot new product. Consider the chagrin of the same researchers as they watched a competitor beat them to the market with the same product because they couldn't market their idea to management.

Technology without marketing ability has become a liability. Trying to implement technology without first marketing it to your corporation is like winking at someone in the dark: You know what you're doing, but no one else does.

Chapter 5

Why IS Is Not a Cheeseburger

In the long run, men hit only what they aim at.

—*Henry David Thoreau*

Marketing cheeseburgers is, admittedly, a lot easier than marketing your IS organization's products and services. The cheeseburger is something tangible. People can see it, smell it, taste it, hold it in their hands. Plus the fact that they really need the product (or its equivalent). People have to eat.

Intangibles, on the other hand, are a lot tougher to market. Insurance, financial planning, reducing the federal deficit, and the rationale behind tax reform all have two common traits:

1. The client can't see, touch, smell, taste, or hear them.
2. More important, because they're intangibles, it's more difficult to appreciate the benefits they confer. The client, therefore, often has the perception that it's something he or she can do without. (No client ever died from postponing a systems application for three months.)

As a rule, intangibles get lower priority. IS products and services are such intangibles. Not the hardware and software, of course, but what you are really marketing to your clients, which is the positive effect these tools can have on their ability to do a better job for the company and for themselves, too.

A client can touch a computer, get noseprints on the monitor, spill coffee on a floppy disk, get peanut butter in the disk drive. But again, the hardware and software are just the tools. The purpose of all your technology is to improve your clients' ability to manage relationships with customers, vendors, employees, and any other audience significant to them.

The more intangible the product, the more important it is for you to have specific marketing goals. Such goals are important because, on the most basic level, if you don't know where you're going, it can be awfully hard to get there. In fact, we can almost guarantee that you will end up somewhere else, probably someplace not of your choosing.

When developing goals, too many people fall into the vagueness trap. Stating that "IS will improve your performance" is worse than useless. It has as much behavioral impact on the client as "Have a nice day." A goal of such nonspecific cotton candy gives no indication of the all-important how and when.

The classic example of effective goal setting came from President John F. Kennedy. When the nation was stunned by a series of Soviet successes in space, President Kennedy wanted to reassert U.S. supremacy in space exploration. To do this, he did not declare "we'll be Number One." Instead, in May 1961, the President committed the United States to landing a manned spacecraft on the moon "before this decade is out." Nothing vague about that. It stated exactly what the United States was going to do and gave a deadline for getting it done.

This was not your ordinary commitment. It required building a series of launch vehicles—the Apollo series—each of which had 6 million components that required a functional reliability of 99.9999+ percent. But the specific goal allowed the men and women working on the space program to break this goal down into millions of individual tasks that could then be scheduled and completed. Result: on July 20, 1969, the Apollo 11 Lunar Module successfully landed on the moon, ahead of schedule.

Goals and objectives are not pie-in-the-sky abstractions. Instead, they should tell you what to do when you get to work on Monday morning. An IS organization's marketing goals should fall into four categories:

1. *Increase awareness.* Applications will never be used if your clients don't know they exist. But beyond educating clients about specific hardware and software, the IPP's primary responsibility is to make clients (or potential clients) more aware of the IS organization's capabilities. Let them know what you can do and how it can help them in their business.

2. *Generate enthusiasm.* IS people love their technology, yet often fail to communicate their enthusiasm to their clients. We're not talking mindless "Up-with-Computers" cheerleading. But you do have to convey to your clients that they're getting in on a good thing. Like it or not, the power of positive thinking works:

> *Researchers at the University of Maryland found that feeling happy can have a significantly positive impact upon getting problems solved. Good feelings increase the tendency to combine materials in new ways to make connections between apparently unrelated ideas. This happens because the positive state results in "defocused attention." That means we cast off our self-imposed blinders, which limit our ability to see new possibilities. Without these blinders, our minds are more open, which leads to a greater range of results. When both IPP and client are working at this level, good things happen for everyone.*

3. *Provide incentives for use.* If your products and services are to be appreciated, your clients must first have a need for them—and be convinced that they have a need for them. IS products and services must be accepted from within, not imposed from without by IS. That means giving clients a reason to want to use them. This is human nature, basic and universal. As far back as 423 B.C., a character in Aristophanes' Greek comedy *The Clouds* asks, "Where does the bread come from?" Loosely translated into corporatese, this means "What's in it for me?"

Never underestimate the role that self-interest plays in the decision of potential clients to use your products and services (or to do anything else. There are a few Mother Teresas out there, but most of them are not in corporate life.) People will decide to work with you only if doing so benefits them in some way.

> *In 1776, the same year that the self-interest of the American colonies led them to declare their independence from England, Adam Smith, the economist and father of capitalism, held that the great motivator of economic activity was "the uniform, constant and uninterrupted effort of every man to better his condition." And, he added, "It is not from the benevolence of the butcher, the brewer or the baker that we expect our dinner but from their regard to their own interest."*

4. *Maximize client control and decision making.* When Thomas Hobson rented out horses in Cambridge, England, about 400 years ago, he gave his clients only one choice—the horse nearest the door. It was that or nothing at all. His name is still known because of his attitude toward customer service, which has been immortalized in the term "Hobson's choice."

That's a better deal than some IS clients get. They don't even have the option of nothing at all. They are told what technology they will use. Period. Since shotgun weddings rarely make for happy marriages, it's no surprise that IS often finds itself engaged in guerilla warfare with the people it should be helping. If your clients feel that they have had a say in the decision-making process, that their input received serious consideration, and that they have control over the technology they are using, their learning and acceptance curves skyrocket. And the IPP is no longer viewed as the corporate Darth Vader but as a valued business partner.

If you're not marketing to the rest of the corporation, the IS organization embodies only the dark side of the force.

Chapter 6

What Makes a
Good Marketer?

*A good listener is not only popular everywhere, but after a while
he/she gets to know something.*

—Wilson Mizner

To succeed at marketing, an IPP needs three sets of skills—
technical, business, and interpersonal.

Technical skills are the knowledge of computers and IS that
the IPP brings to the job. In addition to technology-specific
knowledge, IPPs must also understand the evolution of the
technology they work with.

Business skills encompass an understanding of business
fundamentals, both a knowledge of the specific corporation the
IPP works for and an awareness of trends in the corporation's
industry. All this happens only by getting out from behind the
keyboard and deliberately exposing yourself to the business of
business.

This exposure can be approached in a variety of ways. To
acquire business skills, for example, some IS organizations have
established new positions in an attempt to reach and show clients
that they can communicate with them effectively. Some common
titles are analysts, sponsors, and knowledge engineers. The
purpose is to link someone within IS to the business community
and to add business sense to the IS community.

It's a step, but at best it is merely a band-aid approach to the problem.

My own experience shows that "profession exposure" is the more solid approach. Someone from IS is assigned to live with other departments—actually to become a resident for sixty to ninety days—and he or she observes the very guts of that particular profession—the peaks and valleys, the strengths and weaknesses, what makes it tick! When all the functions have been covered, IS then has a good working knowledge of what goes on in the corporation.

Interpersonal skills involve the ability to interact well with other people in both one-on-one and group situations. Above all, it involves the ability to listen—actively listen.

Let's consider a curious fact about how most IPPs relate to the rest of the corporation. Suppose a group of civilians from several departments are meeting to discuss a problem. IS has been asked to provide technical input. As the IS organization's designated representative, you are on your way to the conference room. As you walk through the halls, you are going over in your mind what you might contribute to this group of people whom you'll be meeting for the first time. What are you bringing to the table?

Your obvious contribution is going to come from the three sets of skills just mentioned. How would you rank them in terms of their importance to the success of the meeting? The typical IPP would rank them in this order: (1) technical skills; (2) business skills; (3) interpersonal skills.

Right? Wrong. Because everyone else at the meeting will rank them in the reverse order. People from the rest of the corporation are not particularly interested in your technical skills. They probably don't understand them anyway but assume you are technically competent or you wouldn't have been asked to represent IS.

More important than your technical skills are your business skills. To the other people at the meeting, if you don't understand the business they are in, you won't understand the problems that will be the topic of the meeting. And that means you won't be able to contribute to the solution.

Unfortunately, IS people tend to be more loyal to their

profession than to their employer. The result is a lot of movement from job to job—from wineries to widget manufacturers—because IS people believe that their technical skills translate to any industry. Although this is true, it does have a downside: Many IS people never learn the business that they are applying their talents to at the moment.

Most important to the other people you are meeting is what kind of human being you are. Are you someone they can work with? Someone who will be an effective part of the team? Someone who will help them find a solution instead of becoming part of the problem? Someone with whom others can form a long-term relationship, complete with trust, reliability, and credibility? Someone who can improve situations by virtue of the mutual interaction?

This is a long way from the inflexible, internal logic of programming languages. Programmers are used to working alone. Sometimes forcing them to work with other people—especially non-IS people—is a surefire method for crashing the system. Can you hack it? Yes, if you remember that you're there to market the IS organization. That means bringing to bear some abilities that usually don't stand out in the résumés of systems people.

Traits of the Good Marketer

A good marketer has some specific abilities—abilities we all possess in different degrees but can certainly further refine. What follows is a partial list of do's and don'ts, one you could probably add to based on your experience and knowledge of the corporation you work in:

- Be multifaceted enough to deal with and understand people in every area of the corporation—and at every level, from the executive suite to the mailroom.

- Appreciate the financial ramifications of each suggested technological application. ("It's going to cost WHAT?" is a question usually asked at the top of a client's voice.) As a general rule, never propose a solution that costs more than the problem.

■ Understand that technology decisions are never made solely on the basis of technological merit. There are always political, competitive, economic, and human factors that can put a spin on each decision.

■ Always attempt to understand and appreciate client behavior.

■ Always seek out better marketing intelligence that will help IS to help the corporation.

■ Help your client to look good in front of his or her boss and management.

■ Cultivate a team atmosphere between IS and the client. Help create a problem-solving approach and attitude.

■ Never promise what can't be delivered. Look at all the facts first, think them through, and don't prejudge.

■ Do more than fill the client's request. When possible, go that extra mile. In fact, you should add value to each client interaction no matter how informal or little that may be.

■ Be human and be yourself. I find that people often try to be somebody they're not. They try to emulate someone they've seen and admired and feel that they will become more effective if they acquire the same qualities. Please think about this seriously. It's better to follow the age-old rule, "Know thyself." The bottom line is that a person is respected for what he or she is. Straying out of character may be good for a professional actor, but it simply doesn't work for most of us.

Explore! Always try to refine your skills. Be proud of what you are; be satisfied with yourself; and you'll find that others are comfortable with you.

Above all, a good marketer is committed to the concept of marketing. Think of it this way: You are a public relations person representing IS every time you meet with a client. Be extremely sensitive to the image of unity you want to establish in this interaction, and strive to project the qualities of professionalism, capability, competence, consistency, and unity.

The H.E.A.R. Model

Communication is the greatest challenge facing any profession in the American corporation. Good communications, in the final analysis, are the key to survival, or success. Communication is everybody's business.

Do not despair! There's a tool that will help you. It involves listening.

We all think we hear well. It's the other guy who doesn't. But let's play a little game: Go way back in your personal data bank, review the acquaintances you've made over your lifetime, and try to list at least three people you consider to be good listeners. (No, the family dog doesn't count!)

Difficult? Yes, it is indeed unusual to find someone who really listens. Now let me ask: Do you respect those you listed? The odds are you definitely do! If I met the people you interact with and asked them this question, would you be on their lists?

Yes, we do respect people who have the decency to listen. The ability to listen is a powerful trait. I have a model that will help you to become a more effective listener. I call it the H.E.A.R. model.

But first a story:

> At one of my seminars a guy explained, "Every evening I watch the TV news, read the paper, and have a drink while dinner is being prepared. The other night my eight-year-old daughter approached me and asked if she could talk with me about her school activities. I had just participated in your H.E.A.R. model exercise that day, so I shut off the TV, laid down the paper, looked her in the eye, and told her 'sure, go ahead.'
>
> She was astounded. She ran to her mother and shouted, 'Mommy, Mommy, something's wrong with Daddy.' "

The point is, we are not, as a population, good listeners. But we need to be. We need to pay more attention to what others are saying, and in so doing we will gain respect.

H.E.A.R. is not just a cute acronym. It's a powerful and effective exercise. Please give it thought as I break it down for you.

The IPP has to do more than merely hear her client. She has to H.E.A.R. the client. This is a four-step process so revolutionary and simple that it's hard to believe a formal model is needed:

1. *Hear*. Physically hear exactly what is said.
2. *Empathize*. Have feeling for what the other person is trying to explain.
3. *Analyze*. Take time to reason it out.
4. *Respond*. Answer all the issues and cover all the bases.

What exactly is meant by these key words?

Hear

Block out external noise and internal arguing. The external noise is easier. Close the door to the office. Forward your telephone calls. Don't tolerate interruptions. There are other kinds of "noise" that should also be eliminated. It's virtually impossible to hold a serious meeting in a high-traffic area—a busy cafeteria, for instance. Besides the noise level, there are too many visual distractions. Taking the steps necessary to eliminate such interruptions communicates to the client that what he has to say is important to you.

Shutting down the internal arguing requires more discipline. It's also more important because internal noise is more distracting—and more treacherous—than the external variety. That's because shutting our minds to our own thoughts is harder than shutting a door. The problem is that while people talk at 150 words a minute, our brains can process 300 words a minute. During any conversation, half of our mental capacity goes unused. What happens with that other half?

Some people use it to figure out how they are going to respond to what the other person is saying. In fact, people like this are probably only listening with 5 percent of their brains. The rest is spinning like crazy because they believe that what they have to say back is more important than what the client is saying. We all know people like this. It's so obvious that they're hearing only a fraction of what we are saying. Their minds are too busy trying to find a way to butt back into the conversation (and dominate it, of course).

To such people, a conversation isn't an exchange of ideas; rather, it's an opportunity to impress the other person. While few people are quite this blatant, all of us are a little guilty of such behavior. It's time to quit it. It's much more important—and effective—to focus on what the client is saying. Ignoring input is just bad DP.

Empathize

Truly put yourself in the client's moccasins. Think long-term and consider more than your immediate organizational turf. The application you are discussing is a technological response to pressure. What's the source of that pressure? The client's boss? The competition? Ambition? Profit and loss considerations? Job security? Fear of your technology? Please note that I'm not necessarily asking you to sympathize with the client—that is, to see things his or her way. But even if you totally disagree with the client, you can still empathize.

People do what they do for reasons. Their reasons may be rational, emotional, or completely off-the-wall, but there are reasons. Even psychotics have reasons for their behavior. The problem is that their reasons are unsuited to the real world.

Writers of whodunits call this motive. Understanding that motive is empathy. It's simply the attempt to grasp what your clients are feeling and why they feel that way. Understand their motivation and you have a better chance of being able to help them. Unless you get inside the client's skin, you are working at a disadvantage in trying to find a mutually acceptable technological solution.

Analyze

Use your analytical skills to find the proper solution and the approach to implementing that solution. Don't make the common mistake of deciding on the answer before you even know the question. Widen your horizons to look at the problem from all angles and from a broader prospective. Ask the client for feedback. Then, and only then, do you analyze.

Respond

Always respond, even if the answer is "I don't know." Never leave anything hanging. But before you respond, hear, empathize, and analyze first.

After all, don't we base our own evaluation of people's intelligence and concern on their willingness to listen to us?

But we shouldn't feel pressured into responding too quickly. In normal interactions, it has been estimated that there can be a buffer time of up to two minutes of pure listening before the conversation reaches the awkward stage. That grace period gives us the appropriate amount of time to formulate our thoughts and respond to a question. It's much better to say it right than to say it quickly and superficially.

Just relax, sit back, hear your client out, and let him voice all his opinions. Don't make over-hasty judgments; don't get hooked emotionally or personally; just listen to what he is telling you. Listen attentively, paraphrase the issue, and clarify it. Better to ask a "dumb" question now than to leave with a misunderstanding and blow the whole project later. You will gain more respect for yourself and greater appreciation for your services when the client feels his needs have been understood, and the results prove it.

The two-minute buffer I mentioned is seemingly contrary to the popular belief that the pause is awkward in American business. I'm reminded of a story in which a pause was responsible for a positive result:

A young applicant at an interview was offered the job and a higher salary than she had ever dreamed of. She was dumbfounded, speechless. The interviewer misinterpreted the pause and said, "Well, I can sweeten that by $3,000. Would that do it for you?"

I can't promise this kind of reward for your silence. But I can guarantee an increase of respect for you from your clients. Just think about it in positive terms.

The H.E.A.R. model has been test-proven, and it will work for you too!

Chapter 7

Gearing Up
for Marketing

The beginning is the most important part of the work.
—Plato
(4th century B.C.)

He who has begun has half done. Dare to be wise; begin!
—Horace
(1st century B.C.)

Just do it.
—Nike
(Quite recently)

Before the IS organization can help its clients, it must first get its own house in order. IS may be a tight, professional technology operation, but that doesn't mean it's ready for internal marketing. To evaluate how well your IS group is performing as a marketing force for technology, run through the true/false quiz included as the Appendix. If you do not do well on this test, some team building might be a good place to start. The IS marketing philosophy begins with individuals, but it is based on a team concept, as shown in Figure 7-1.

As I travel around the country taking the pulse of business-people, asking about their impressions of IS in general, I'm sorry to report that we are not known as a "we" kind of team. I don't

Figure 7-1.   The MIS team-based marketing philosophy.

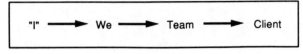

think we have purposely encouraged this feeling, or that we are bad people, or anything of the sort. I just feel that in IS we tend to do things individually. For example, the following statements are common among IS people:

> "I will take care of that problem."
> "I will turn it over to Joe, who is the statistical analysis systems expert."
> "I will forward it to Mary, who knows PS-2 better than anybody else."

Within our organization we do pride ourselves on our individual technical knowledge base, and we know exactly who should handle a certain application. But doesn't it work against our IS organizational image when clients go directly to Joe or Mary? And they will do so if they think of us only as a collection of individuals, not as a team. It's only human nature.

We must change our image to a *we* department. *We* are a team!

> "We will handle it."
> "We will work on it."
> "We will give you the answer."

Ideally, the IPP (the "I" of Figure 7-1) gets the initial request from the client. The client and the IPPs then review the best approach to the problem. The team (the IS organization) provides the resources needed for a solution. The client request is satisfied.

Building the Team

Before such a client-oriented process can take place, however, the IS executive has to build an IS team responsive to this approach. This should not be a hot news flash. One of management's principal roles is to create teams. This starts with taking a serious approach to hiring, which entails looking hard for the correct balance between the job need and the candidate's blend with both management philosophy and staff culture.

Recruitment

To build a marketing-oriented IS team, the IPP must first have a tough recruitment screening process. Your objectives and customer service philosophy must be clearly understood and matched. Personal characteristics that indicate a direction toward customer satisfaction must be coupled with a problem-solving attitude, a desire to apply friendly, sensitive communication skills, and a true ability and desire to listen.

People on the IS team should clearly show patience, flexibility, and enthusiasm for their work and possess the high energy required to keep pace and the discretion to reserve judgment until all aspects of a problem are understood.

While the corporation's human resources people can help in the initial screening process, it is still the IPP who has the final say. How do you know that a candidate is as good as he says he is? The résumé is no help. Even if the job candidate can't fake a good résumé, there are a lot of professional services that will do it for him. And no one will list as a reference anyone who would be so unkind as to mention flaws in his or her character.

You have to read between the lines, hear what the candidate is not saying. And even then it's a crapshoot. Not until after the hiree's first day on the job do you know what you have. That's why it's important for every new IS member to know exactly what's expected of him or her and to be familiar with the management philosophy employed—and why—in their transactions with the client community.

You must have standards in place and measure the performance of each team member against those standards. No manager with unscrambled circuits likes to play the heavy. It's always easier—and a lot more fun—to reward excellence than to come down on nonperformers. But letting one person's job performance slide—for whatever reason—will undermine your group's morale as badly as will a lack of recognition for good work. A person who doesn't measure up should be told that perhaps his career would prosper better elsewhere.

Another key ingredient of a successful team is a leader who's loyal to team members, who should complement rather than mirror the leader's abilities. A common failing of interviewers is to hire only people of similar backgrounds or attitudes. This can sometimes yield bizarre results, as when a Yul Brynner-like corporate executive refused to hire anyone who wasn't at least six feet tall.

The problem with this approach is the inherent flaw behind many forms of discrimination: You miss out on the advantages that come from having a broad range of collective experience. You end up with a team that, at best, can do one thing well. When faced with a problem, this team tends to respond with whatever it does best . . . which may not be what's needed.

Another executive had an even more interesting and dysfunctional idiosyncrasy: She was afraid that a stellar performance by a subordinate would make her look bad. As a result, she wouldn't hire anyone who knew more about her field than she did. Since she didn't know much, the result was fairly predictable: The average level of competence within the department went down. Eventually, so did the exec.

H. S. M. Burns, the late president of Shell Oil, once outlined a better approach to management. For him, "A good manager is a man who isn't worried about his own career, but rather about the careers of those who work for him. My advice: Don't worry about yourself. Take care of those who work for you and you'll float to greatness on their achievements."

When an IS manager doesn't take care of his team, everyone floats, but not to greatness.

John was an MIS specialist with superb technical abilities. When he was Peter-Principled into managing a team put together to tackle a critical systems project, he simply refused to manage the people now working for him. Instead, he stayed behind the closed door of his office, doing his own piece of the project, while his team floundered for lack of direction. Eventually John was demoted, but not before he had blown crucial deadlines. To this day, within that company the reputation of the entire IS organization still suffers from that fiasco. And to this day, a hurt and bewildered John still doesn't understand what he did wrong.

The Care and Feeding of Team Members

Good people and the right team structure bring good ideas into focus. But a good team must be carefully nurtured and supported by the IS exec. The nature of that support can be described as "The Five Cs of Management": (1) comfort, (2) clarification, (3) confrontation, (4) control, and (5) celebration.

1. *Comfort.* We all have rotten days, the kind where we wish we had stayed in bed, curled up in a fetal position under the protection of the blankets. When it happens, knowing that someone understands goes a long way toward helping you to dust yourself off and hurl yourself back into the fray. A good manager offers this type of comfort. But please, don't misinterpret this. "Buddy-buddy" is not what I mean!

2. *Clarification.* Because IS people are in a fast-paced environment, emotions sometimes run high. These high emotions complicate client relationships, internal IS relationships, and the problem-solving process. At this point, the IS exec must get all parties into neutral corners until emotions are cooled down and disentangled from work issues. The manager must bring clarity to the situation.

3. *Confrontation.* Conflict can be healthy, but it's important to make sure that the issues are confronted in a positive way. Never attack. Backing someone up against a wall serves only to escalate the conflict. A person with no way out will only go for the throat . . . yours. This doesn't mean that we should avoid logical and necessary confrontations or feel guilty about them. Confrontation is considered one of the most awkward situations faced by American management, and the tendency is to avoid it, to smooth things over. But we have to realize that a smooth sea will inevitably become rough at times. We just can't steer around it.

We need to become better confronters, not for the sake of

affixing blame but in order to strive for balance and to clear the air. For example, in confronting an IS employee on the issue of teamwork, be firm, but leave some hope. You might say:

> "If your attitude doesn't change, I feel strongly that it will affect your growth here."
>
> "We have a well-defined work load in this department and you must contribute your full share."
>
> "Your interaction with clients is not up to our teamwork standards. It needs improvement."

In other words, be direct, honest, and firm, but do not strip a person of his or her self-esteem.

4. *Control*. Control is a large part of the management function, but there are also dangers in overcontrol. I believe we have to relinquish some of this control once we have achieved a true feeling of teamwork within the IS organization.

Dr. George Laberwicz of Boston University, an accomplished pilot, states that the worst thing pilots do is to overcontrol the plane. The plane is made to fly and if you let it, it will!

It's the same with a team. If all members are well-instituted, well-instructed, and well-balanced, the team will fly on its own. You can leave it on automatic pilot!

5. *Celebration*. Now that we are comfortable, the issues are clarified, the confrontations have been worked out, and everything is under control, it's time to celebrate.

In our daily grind we are too apt to dwell on the negative— the things we didn't accomplish or didn't do efficiently. The good manager has to recognize the positive things as well and react positively to team members' efforts.

Perhaps this involves taking someone who has performed "above and beyond the call of duty" out to lunch or dinner. Perhaps it's something as simple as sitting back late on a Friday afternoon and saying, "Hey gang! Have a good weekend. We deserve it!"

Recognition

You can build up team morale via informalities, or you can establish some regular reward programs. These can be:

- *Conditional*. Promising a reward for completing a specific task conditioned on the outcome of that task.
- *On-the-spot*. Giving a spontaneous award of appreciation for a job well done.
- *Surprise*. Planning almost any kind of award in recognition of an outstanding accomplishment.* The cost can range from expensive to free and should be tailored to the size of the accomplishment and company norms. Ideas include:
  —Gift certificates
  —Cash awards
  —Thank-you notes via electronic mail
  —Featuring the accomplishment on bulletin boards or in the company newsletter
  —Naming an employee of the month or birthday of the month
  —Movie or concert tickets
  —Award banquets
  —Discounts in the company store
  —A day off or even a Monday morning off from work
  —Coming in late on a predetermined day
  —A new job title
  —A special parking spot
  —Choice of an educational seminar or conference
  —Hanging a photo of the employee for recognition

Recognition should go beyond the IS organization. If a programmer does an especially good job for the accounting department, let the head of accounting know. A letter of commendation in the employee's personnel file never hurts either.

Protection

The flip side of giving external recognition is shielding your team from external criticism. A good boss protects team members when

---

*One company actually has a formal teddy bear program. A significant accomplishment is followed by a box mailed to the employee's home. In the box is a small teddy bear. No letter. No announcement by management at work. But you had better believe that the next day everyone knows that the employee got a teddy bear. The effect on morale is impressive.

mistakes are made. This does not mean that you cover up for them or let them get away with it. It does mean that any criticism or disciplinary action involving an IS staff member must come directly from you, that person's boss. No bricks lobbed in from elsewhere in the organization can be allowed. Besides, it's your area of responsibility, so it's your mistake too. The worst sort of corporate wimp is the boss who counters criticism from on high by laying the blame at the feet of someone on his staff. That does wonders for organizational loyalty!

On the other hand, when staff members know that they have the freedom to make mistakes, that is the best guarantee of quality. People work better when they don't have to watch their backs constantly and when they don't have someone always looking over their shoulder.

The serious point I want to make here is that all this must be done with honesty and sensitivity. If not sincere, it will be seen as a "gimme" and be demoralizing. The type of management I have been describing creates an atmosphere of honesty and encourages service-oriented staff members, willing to accommodate and fill requirements, knowing they have support behind them. To the client, this in itself is a form of marketing.

Chapter 8

Creating a Client Attitude

You can't put the same shoe on every foot.

—Publilius Syrus
(1st century B.C.*)*

Many IPPs would be much more comfortable with the concept of marketing their IS organization internally if it didn't require them to deal with clients.

I frequently ask this question during a seminar: "Are you people kind of people? Do you like working with people?" I'll never forget that at one seminar in Miami after asking this question, one student said, "Not me, I hate people. Leave me alone with my terminal; I can get much more work done without people interactions." Well, I knew I had my work cut out. He was a great guy and after a few days he saw the value to himself and others of interacting differently. And he did.

A number of studies have shown that people who are attracted to computers in the first place tend to be somewhat introverted. They prefer being behind their keyboards precisely because it keeps them away from people interactions and other nonprogrammable annoyances.

Tom was such a person. One of the best DP people in the company, he prided himself on the quality of his work. He also

59

thought that as long as he produced excellent work, people would leave him alone. When they didn't, he ignored them. The door to his office was always closed. He never returned phone calls, even from high-ranking executives.

Eventually, this rather blatant reality avoidance caught up with Tom in ways large and small. When the company installed a new phone system, instead of the "executive phone" and the higher-status extension ending in zero, to which his rank as a department head entitled him, he got a clerical phone and an extension ending in three.

Big deal, right? No. Even had he known he'd been slighted, which he didn't because he never left his office except to go to the coffee machine or the washroom, it wouldn't have mattered to Tom: He never used the phone anyway. And status meant as little to him as pearls to a pig. But Tom was also unaware that he was paying a bigger price—loss of credibility within his own department and throughout the company.

The people who worked for Tom saw what was happening and tried to cover for him as much as they could. They returned phone calls, represented him at meetings, and made excuses for why he wasn't available. All this eventually built up a lot of hostility toward Tom because his behavior was interfering with his colleagues' jobs and hurting the department's reputation. Clients with projects began bypassing Tom's department because trying to reach him was more trouble than it was worth. Some of the projects went to other departments, others to outside vendors. The quality work that Tom took so much pride in was now being handled by others. When Tom was finally asked to leave, he was totally shocked. He left behind a department that had to rebuild its credibility from scratch.

Tom—and his name is legion—made the mistake of believing that the "product" produced by IS was a physical thing, hardware and software. It's not. Instead, the real product that IS produces is an array of technical, economic, psychological, and personal relationships between marketeer and clients. This entails treating clients as partners, even if IS people have to go outside their own personal zone of comfort to do so.

Introverts like Tom simply don't understand the much broader zone of comfort exhibited by the true extrovert, like that created by those social butterflies who can walk up to a total stranger and say, "Hi! I'm Charlie. How do you like me so far?"

For the true systems introvert, this behavior is as out of place as a Tupperware party in the Vatican. IPPs would rather volunteer for root canal work than go outside their comfort zone. (It should be pointed out here that I am not making fun of systems introverts. Don't be fooled by the fact that as an author I commit—with alarming frequency—outrageously extroverted acts such as getting up in front of a roomful of total strangers to give speeches and seminars. Beneath this moderately manic exterior is a hard-core introvert.)

Introverts should be encouraged by the fact that many top performers in America are not gregarious individuals. It is not at all unusual for Hollywood stars who shine in front of the camera to hide from the limelight when not on the set.

This is also true of some professional athletes. There are some, of course, who revel in the notoriety; but there are others who shy away from the publicity and the hype—perhaps like IS people.

In the case of the reticent stars of screen and sport, we could say that it's coincidental, but perhaps unfortunate, that their particular talent puts them constantly in front of an audience. But they have learned to accept the role and it hasn't detracted from their skill.

The role of the shy and introverted IS person could be compared with this. The deep thought required by the exercise of technology lends itself to introversion. But try to think of the IS room as a stage or playing field; when the lights go off, be yourself. Business after all is a drama.

More on the positive side, I truly believe that IS people rank very high in self-starting, energy, and precision. If you have any doubts about IPPs being self-starters, ask yourself:

- How often do you work more than an eight-hour day?
- How often do you go into work early or on weekends?
- How often do you find yourself resolving a technical or systems implementation issue while showering or supposedly listening to your significant other?

Most IS professionals I have met over the years are self-starters. They constantly want to resolve issues or find the proper technical approach to a system and put a lot of effort into attaining that goal.

It should also be pointed out that the people who become managers within the IS organization probably have a little more of the extrovert in them than the average IPP person. Many are promoted to supervisory positions precisely because they are seen to have more in the way of people skills than the majority of their DP brethren. If IPPs can deal with people within the IS organization, it's not that much of a stretch for them to deal with people in the rest of the corporation.

The hard part is for IPPs to convince themselves of the contribution they can make to the company. It's generally known that IPPs do not understand their true value or how to state it. Perhaps the antidote is some commonsense ideas as to how to develop a positive mental attitude about the IS profession and the value IPPs provide to their clients. In marketing the IS organization internally, the emphasis should be on having your clients keep you "in sight and in mind." How? By applying what should be some basic managerial traits.

The following are simple ways in which you can help change your approach to client interactions:

- *Design a long-term IS strategy that has impact.*

- *Commit yourself to adding value to every transaction.* This applies to all professional contacts, formal or informal: phone conversations, meetings, presentations, training sessions, seminars, even a brief exchange in an elevator or restroom.

- *Apply your "standards" only after you fully understand your client's needs.*

- *Master the art of asking questions to achieve mutual understanding.* After you ask a question, STOP! The best listeners have a genuine desire to learn from others. And always, always apply the H.E.A.R. Model.

- *Bring your technical and marketing skills to everyone.* That means people you like, people you're neutral about, people you don't like, even that bozo on the seventh floor. You're not marketing to help individuals. You're marketing to advance the good of the IS organization as a true asset to the corporation.

Confronting a Difficult Client Interaction

You're convinced. You now believe in the need for the IS organization to market itself internally. You go to your client meeting . . . and find yourself facing a client group so hostile that it looks like the scene in the movie *Frankenstein* in which the angry peasants march on the castle with pitchforks and torches.

"OK, dispensers of wisdom," you mutter as you get your back to the wall and slowly edge your way toward the door, "now what do I do?"

This can actually be a window of opportunity. I can tell you story after story of initially very difficult clients who later became great supporters and even sponsors of IS.

If this occurs, don't get hooked emotionally and don't take it personally. Instead, work towards making a deposit in the bank of human relationships. Actually invite the client to tell you more. Let him vent his rage, respect his feelings. Listen sincerely and don't promise a quick fix. You will soon gain an ally.

Leaving a client dissatisfied simply isn't acceptable—not if there's any way to avoid it. First, in purely pragmatic terms, it hurts you and your IS organization. Look at car buyers for a moment. Do you know how many people a satisfied car owner tells about his car? Eight. How many does a dissatisfied owner tell? Twenty-two. That's just human nature. If you walk away from a problem, you're leaving behind more than one negative opinion. You're leaving behind someone who will go out of his way to spread that negative opinion of your IS organization. A better approach is to "cool off" an angry client. Follow these guidelines:

- *Keep yourself calm and relaxed.* If you blow up too, it will only serve to escalate the conflict.

- *Give the client a chance to vent.* Sometimes all a person wants is the opportunity to get something off his chest. But your client may need this opportunity before the two of you can work out the problem. The advice of Lord Chesterfield, the eighteenth-century British statesman, still stands: "Patience is the most necessary quality for business; many a man would rather you heard his story than grant his request."

- *Empathize with the client.* Saying "Hey, buddy, I got my problems too!" is not what the client wants to hear right now . . . even if it's true.

- *Restate the client's concern.* For communication to be truly effective, it has to be two-way. Your client needs feedback. Let him know that you really listened and understand the problem.

- *Find some area of agreement with the client.* "The entire project's a disaster!" is tough to deal with. Break the problem down into bite-size pieces. Find which aspects are acceptable to the client. This accomplishes several things. It makes the client realize that the situation may not be quite so disastrous after all. The analysis that goes into breaking down the problem to find areas of agreement may in itself pinpoint the real problem. In any case, the remaining areas of disagreement may be easier to tackle now that they're separated out. Finally, the fact that you are able to reach agreement in some areas helps rebuild the sense of partnership necessary to working together.

- *Transfer or delay any confrontation.* If none of these nostrums works, stall for time. Promise to get back to the client next week, tomorrow, in an hour. Any kind of delay gives the client a chance to cool off and gives you some time to figure out what's going on and what you can do about the problem.

- *Confront the client.* Nobody likes confrontation (except certain TV talk show hosts); however, sometimes you just have to deal with the issue then and there—but always with sensitivity.

When Conflict Is Inevitable

Even war has rules. If conflict with a client is inevitable, approach it as a professional:

- *View the other person as human.* We all tend to think in terms of black and white, the good guys versus the bad guys, us versus them. In fact, most of what passes for reality is this huge, amorphous, gray marshmallow. Forget that and suddenly the person you're arguing with grows another head and one big eye in the middle of each forehead. When you start to view the client as an ogre, step back and lighten up. Life's not that simple.

- *If the IS organization is to achieve credibility within the corporation, you must meet the client's needs as well as your own.* A shared human problem is a lot easier to resolve than open conflict.

- *Keep your mind open to the client's suggestions.* There's more than one solution to any problem. Admitting that the other person has good ideas is a sign of strength, not weakness. It also helps rebuild the partnership.

- *Always explain exactly what you mean.* Define your terms. Clients need to know what you mean, not guess at what they suppose you might mean. Time after time needless conflicts arise because the people involved are attaching different meanings to the same word or using different terms to mean the same thing. When the dust settles, you might have a serious case of agreement.

- *Be realistic.* What do you have to gain or lose in this conflict? Not everything is worth going to the wall for. Our personal definition of maturity is knowing which battles are worth fighting.

- *Be goal-oriented.* Your overriding purpose is to promote the best interests of the company, the client, and the IS organization. Always think long-term. Is it worth winning the battle with the client if it means losing the war?

Chapter 9

Role Models

We are what we pretend to be, so we must be careful about what we pretend to be.

—Kurt Vonnegut, Jr.

Ask any frontline grunt whether he'd rather be up there walking point because someone told him to, or back where the decisions are made. In a less dramatic context, to be sure, that's really the choice IS has to make: either to be a management function, or to be among those who just accept their marching orders.

The IS organization's importance and level of influence in a company can vary widely. Effective marketing of IS services and of the benefits IS provides can make the difference between an IS organization that is merely an administrative function that carries out orders and one that is an influential key player in the organization.

The IPP should realize that the benefits of marketing will not be achieved by making marketing just another item on a to-do list along with budgeting, monthly reports, and training plans. Marketing is a basic orientation, a state of mind, a constant frame of reference through which the IPP views the world. Marketing is giving constant attention to the questions, "Who is my client?" and "What services can I offer that client?"

The IPP should impress upon the IS staff that the people who come in are clients, people whose needs the IS staff is there to serve. Everyone within the corporate hierarchy and across every department should be treated professionally and with genuine concern. The IPP should not take this for granted, especially with new staff members. Their training should include coaching on how to greet and deal with clients who come into IS.

A consistent problem-solving approach helps IS develop a reputation for professionalism and an orientation to client problems.

To generate ideas about how to market IS, it is useful to see IS through two analogies: (1) the IS organization as a public relations firm; and (2) the IS organization as a consulting firm. Each model can lead to new ways of looking at IS and to appropriate ways of marketing the IS organization.

The Public Relations Model

Public relations, like marketing, may have negative connotations for some IPPs who have risen through the technical ranks. There is a negative side to public relations—excessive hype, unrealistic promises, smoothing over failures or troublesome areas. These have no place in the IS marketing effort. (In fact, they have no place in public relations either, as PR professionals will be the first to tell you.)

What is useful in the PR model is its basic goal of building an awareness of services offered and taking advantage of opportunities to establish and enhance the IS organization's image as a professional, effective function meeting real business needs.

Consider for a moment how a public relations pro would look at the challenge of marketing your IS organization. You have an image of your IS team. Your people are good and they do good work. Now if everyone else in the corporation saw your IS team the way you do, you wouldn't need to market yourselves. You'd have clients lined up around the block.

Unfortunately, the rest of your company may not see you this way. Other departments may have a different image of IS. That image may be based on bad information or, more likely, lack of information (or remember the legend left by Tom in Chapter 8). The job of public relations is to reconcile these two images.

Figure 9-1.   The public relations model for IS.

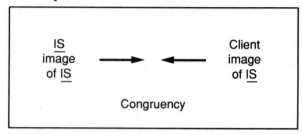

When the images become congruent (see Figure 9-1), when the rest of the corporation sees you the way you see yourselves, IS will be functioning as an integral part of corporate strategy.

Please note that when PR professionals talk about image, they do not mean some superficial veneer laid on like wallpaper to cover over something negative. In public relations, image equals credibility. Thus the purpose of public relations and of marketing is to establish your credibility in the minds of your clients.

To accomplish this, both the PR pro and the IS pro have a variety of communication tools available. (These are discussed in Chapters 14 and 15.) Regardless of the marketing tools used, IPPs should profile their intended clients to ensure that the message and the media specifically address their needs and concerns. Marketing IS to top management in key board meetings requires an entirely different approach from marketing document processing to rank-and-file clerical staff.

Whatever communication tools you use, your message should be consistent and grounded in reality. Why? Because reality is the most important communication. Only 3 percent of the communications others receive from us are in the form of formal communications (printed materials, memos, graphics). Listening? That's only another 7 percent. The biggest contributor by far—90 percent—comes from reality: our actions, products, services, and working conditions.

If our formal communications tell our clients "We love you," but the other 97 percent are a kick in the stomach, guess which message is going to be believed? Sending our clients mutually contradictory messages creates the cognitive dissonance described earlier.

The purpose of public relations is to prevent this kind of credibility gap from arising. But the best PR effort will fail if the reality of the IS organization is the problem. If your reality is positive, however, your IS organization would be well-served by applying some of the skills and qualities of a good public relations person:

- *Writing ability.* No one expects IPPs to be professional writers, but the ability to turn out a concise, interesting, intelligible memo or report never hurt anyone's career. Most corporations offer courses in this area periodically. Sign up! Take a few night courses if need be.
- *Knowledge of a specific business.* Research your company's or client's business hot buttons prior to your first meeting whenever possible.
- *Sensitivity to human relations*—both in dealing with individuals and with corporate politics.
- *An understanding of how behavior is motivated.*
- *Financial sense.* Recognize that IS is probably an overhead to the corporation. Respect clients for seeing IS this way. Although you don't need to defend the dollars, do position the values received for the expenditures wherever possible.
- *Flexibility.* Even the interruptions get interrupted.
- *The ability to manage one's time.*
- *The will to win.* PR is a business of rejection, yet the pros are determined to overcome.
- *Calmness.* In times of crisis, the last thing in the world the IS organization needs is someone like the character described by Canadian humorist Stephen Leacock: "He jumped on his horse and rode off in all directions."
- *Identification with the client.* This is what makes the PR person a true consultant.

The Consulting Model

What does it mean, from a marketing standpoint, to view your IS operation as a consulting firm? First, it means actively perceiving the people and groups in the corporation as clients rather than as people to be supported or trained. This gives the IPP a whole new perspective and can lead to a more innovative, creative application of IS resources to the organization's success.

After all, most IPPs are in the IS field because they see the value of computing and the great potential of these tools and methods to improve productivity and profitability, to respond to change, and to affect decision making. Most IPPs advocate this type of change but do not aggressively pursue it.

The entire IS staff, consultants or analysts in particular, should be explicitly trained in a business problem-solving approach that focuses on client needs rather than on products. Such training not only provides the staff with needed skills but also conditions their responses to clients. Consistency in this approach serves as one of the best marketing tools because it helps to develop IS's reputation for professionalism and an orientation to client problems.

For IPPs, one of the most difficult of all tools to acquire is a hard-nosed approach to business results. As one frustrated line manager put it, "I hate going to IS with anything. To them there's no such thing as a little problem. No matter how minor the project, they always want to do the IS equivalent of building the Great Pyramid. Not on my budget. Living with the problem is more cost-effective than their solution."

Admittedly, such criticism may be unfair. The line manager who over the weekend cobbles together a prototype solution on his or her PC can't understand why IS insists that the project will take six weeks. But then the line manager doesn't have to worry about alpha or beta testing and integrating the new system into the corporation's already complex mainframe systems.

A more important factor is how success is measured. It's not up to IS to decide whether or not a particular change is working. Success or failure can be defined only by the client.

That's why it's critical for the IPP to see beyond a project's technical success to the real business results. It requires extra effort in follow-up and some form of measurement of results (usually the hardest part of a project). However, expending the extra effort gives the IPP the best of all marketing tools: a proven track record of business improvements.

If IPPs are to function as consultants, it's important for them to understand the dynamics of consulting.

First of all, let's consider the word *consultant*. The very word brings to mind certain stereotypes. The first definition you might hear, even from highly intelligent people, is, "A consultant is a very high-priced guru who is paid big bucks!"

Here are some other understandings about consultants:

The 50-mile rule: If a company brings in a consultant from more than 50 miles away, he is a big wheel on a large per diem; if they fly him in, he's a king!

A consultant is a person you go to and ask the time. He'll borrow your watch, tell you the time, keep your watch, and send you a bill. Or

There's a bunch of consultants in a room buried up to their necks in cement. What's missing? More cement!

Oh yes, there are some unflattering stereotypes of consultants these days and also a general perception that management tends to listen with more understanding and respect to an outsider than it does to a regular employee. The common guy thinks, "What am I, chopped liver? I've been pointing out these problems for months, but nobody listened. Now this big guru says it and it's accepted."

Well, these are images we'll just have to live with, but what is more important is what you, as an IS person, should think about yourself as a consultant. There's an opportunity for you to bring a new meaning to the word.

Think about it this way: Being consultants means you and me working with everybody else and consulting with each other on a daily basis. Whether you're in IS or in communication with IS, whether you're talking to IS colleagues or those from other business functions, whether you're a programmer/coder, a technical support person, or an end-user environment person, you are actually consulting every day!

That's the kind of consulting I'm talking about: you and your expertise, available, on the scene, ready and willing to be consulted.

Whatever the consultant's field of expertise, the process of clienting remains the same. Consultants are asked to provide information. But how the client asks the question can predetermine the answer. For example, you can ask your child, "Are you going out now?" Or you can ask, "You're not going out now, are you?" In theory, both questions are basically the same. In fact, they will probably get quite different responses.

The same problem arises in dealing with IS clients. A client comes to IS because she is dissatisfied with the information she has been receiving—or not receiving. Or maybe it's a question of the timing or format of that information. Or the impact it's having on business relationships. In any case, the information she wants is the answer to a question she must ask in order to do her job.

For example, the director of sales asks IS to develop a program that will break down sales volume and revenues for a retail product by city and town. No problem. But why does she need that information? It turns out that the product in question is expensive. The sales director thinks that the company could increase sales by focusing a direct mail program at geographic areas in which the product has sold well.

IS could take the easy way out by giving the director exactly what she wants. Or it could go further to provide an even better answer by breaking down sales by ZIP code. It could pinpoint ZIP codes where the product is selling well, use the latest census data to analyze the demographics of people in those ZIP codes, and then use the same census data to target other ZIP codes with similar demographic profiles. Then IS could tell the sales division exactly where to send its direct mail.

For the consultant, the critical issue is always the same: "Is the client asking the right questions?" Because how the questions are asked can influence the shape of the solution. The consultant must ask the client why she is seeking the information and what she intends to do with it. Only when you know this can you help frame the right question. To help solve difficult problems, follow these five steps:

1. Ask the client a series of questions: What have you tried in the past? What were the results? What have you thought about but haven't yet tried? Why? In that any problem is often symptomatic of a larger one, ask: What else isn't going well? If

IS can solve the problem, how will the solution be applied? Will it alleviate or aggravate the larger problem? Will we get wide acceptance for the solution? Can the organization afford the solution?

2. *Give a diagnosis*. The client asks, "Can you help me define the problem? I don't know what's wrong."

3. *Make recommendations*.

4. *Implement or assist in implementing recommendations*.

5. *Build consensus on or commitment to corrective action*. This is necessary to win acceptance for your solutions. To build consensus, you need to know your company's corporate culture. What does it accept and what does it resist? How willing is the company to work on the problem? Will senior management listen? There are endless stories of IS groups getting beaten up pretty badly because they insisted on advocating a solution that, while technically perfect, was politically unacceptable to the rest of the organization. In such situations, IS may have goodness, truth, and beauty on its side but will get shot out of the water anyway.

A good consultant's client orientation means using the Socratic method of questioning clients to find the answers. Good consultants generally do not work out the solution themselves but help their clients to work it out. They also give away ownership of the solution to the client. The consultant's job is not that of getting credit but of giving it. Besides, the higher truth is that we could not give credit unless it was ours to give.

Finally, a good consultant teaches clients how to solve the problem themselves, so they won't have to keep coming back to re-solve the same problem. In short, a good consultant is always trying to work himself out of a job. After all, that's the best way to get invited back.

Chapter 10

The Strategic Plan

Abbott: Where did you get your good judgment?
Costello: From experience.
Abbott: Where did you get your experience?
Costello: From bad judgment.

—Bud Abbott and Lou Costello

It's not enough anymore to use yesterday's experience as a basis for dealing with tomorrow's problems. Corporate survival requires strategy, which can be defined as how the corporation will arrive at a desired position in a predicted future world. This statement has two serious implications for IPPs:

1. That IS should have some assumptions about the shape of the future in which the company will be operating.

2. That if IS is not plugged into the corporation's strategic plan, IS will be out of step with its environment. This is a high-risk strategy for any element within an organization. Since the most important knowledge issue for managers is to know how much they don't know, it's vital to get a handle on the environment, the strategic planning, and the risk.

Information Management

As spies have always known, information is a salable commodity. More important, information is power. Within the corporation, information is easily politicized. As keepers of the information, IS can be caught in an uncomfortable political role. However, the transition to end-user computing is changing that. The new source of power is not money in the hands of a few but information in the hands of many.

The ability to tap into information gives many groups the right or at least the opportunity to challenge the establishment's official views. This explains why the Soviet Union traditionally has been somewhat schizophrenic about the computer revolution. The Kremlin knew that its economy desperately needed the technology, but it was equally desperate to limit access to it. Sorry, comrades. As *perestroika* has shown, you can't have it both ways.

These are not the only issues, of course. Organizations face increased competitive pressures (both national and international), continuing deregulation, the growing interdependence of institutions, employees' changing attitudes toward work and leisure, the emergence of the postindustrial society, the strengthening of pluralism and individualism, the need for day care, a deteriorating infrastructure, a deteriorating educational system, unresolved equal opportunity issues, and so on. Make your own list. The important thing is that management and, therefore, IS will have to deal with them if they want their organizations to succeed. That's where strategy comes in.

Strategy: Putting the Vision in Place

Chapter 9 discussed your image of your IS organization. The corporation as a whole also has an image of itself and a vision of where it wants to be in the future. That vision is—or should be—the organization's mission. Strategy is how the corporation plans on getting itself to that objective, the vision of itself in the future.

The word strategy has become faddish among those who prefer to be trendy. At its most extreme are the pseudo-strategic planners who could mess up a two-car funeral. Because these types prefer process to results, they have totally distanced themselves from the company's messy, hands-on business of earning a living.

Once you start believing that the purpose of planning is just to produce reports, not a sparrow falleth from the heavens that isn't the subject of thirty-seven memos and twenty-eight meetings. The poet T. S. Eliot's "J. Alfred Prufrock," who measured out his life with coffee spoons while wondering "Do I dare?. . . Do I dare?" was probably a strategic planner reduced to paralysis by analysis.

Almost two and a half centuries ago the moralist George Savile wisely observed, "He that leaveth nothing to chance will do few things ill, but he will do very few things." So the disease is not new, although its current state of contagion is. If strategy has been reduced to a mere buzzword, that doesn't obviate the need for it. A number of factors demand that a continuing emphasis be placed on effective strategy:

- Business today is exposed to a much greater range of pressures.

- The payouts are much shorter, with everyone wanting their money back sooner.

- Improved communications mean that everyone wants information on what you're doing and they want it much faster.

- The competition is worldwide and bare-knuckled.

- To compete, corporations need an increasingly faster reaction time.

- Organizations are much larger and more complex and require more money to feed them.

- Broad-based changes in social and business attitudes continue apace.

- Management is divorced from ownership. This entails a broader obligation on the part of managers because it's not their money.

- Even if management did not feel this obligation, the fact that shareholders will sell out to the first corporate raider who tenders a higher price per share should help focus management on taking care of business.

- There are two kinds of change that a corporation brings about itself. The first is cheap and easy to undo if you make a mistake; you simply change the brand of paper clips or paper towels you purchase. The second, the Big-League Blunder, is very hard and very expensive to negate once you put your foot in it. The technology changes brought about by IS tend to be in the latter category, making it critical that IS get it right the first time.

Consider something on the minor end of IS headaches. Several years ago, Pitney Bowes was upgrading to a more advanced version of Lotus 1-2-3. No big deal, right? It turned out that bean counters at various Pitney Bowes divisions found that they couldn't combine spreadsheets because different versions of the software had been used. Result: Pitney Bowes's director of planning and information resources went outside the IS organization and hired a consultant to straighten out the problem.

Now multiply that minute problem by the thousands of computer hardware and software products available. Then square it and cube it by the increasing complexity of systems. All this boils down to two words: more risk.

In a world that remains chaotic and unpredictable, we need strategic planning to cope with that risk. Without planning, we only react to an unpredictable world. We are always trapped in a defensive mode, operating from a position of weakness in response to the unanticipated. Planning, on the other hand, offers us options. With planning, we can decide what's right for the corporation and act from a position of strength to shape events.

Before that can happen, we have to have some clue as to what might be coming down the pike, headed our way. Lord Bowen, a nineteenth-century British jurist, defined hard work as answering yes or no on imperfect information. That's where forecasting comes in.

Predicting as the Focus of Strategic Planning

Predictability is at the heart of profitability. The purpose of forecasting is to help the corporation crystallize the predictability of events and the corporation's possible responses to those events.

However, before you make any forecasts, consider some pitfalls. Guard against them by doing the following:

- *Double-check your assumptions.* Many forecasts crash because the world has changed. (How many IS budgets were blown when the shortage of microchips jacked up the cost of hardware?)
- *Hedge your bets.* Don't get locked into just one or two sets of assumptions. One planner who made that mistake was General Custer. It's a curious world out there, one that bears a greater resemblance to the twilight zone than to the movements of a Swiss watch.
- *Determine if your focus is too narrow.* Step back, maybe throw your assumptions out the window. A larger frame of reference might help you to see the problem from a different perspective. The new definition may point to a better solution.
- *Don't get caught up in your own technology.* The movie *Tron* was about a man who got trapped in his computer. He almost didn't survive. The focus should be on the information, not the delivery system.
- *Perform reality checks.* You're smart but you're not perfect. Everyone in a position of authority needs at least one staff person who can be trusted to tell the boss, "You're wrong." If you don't have someone playing this role for you, appoint one trusted staff member to the position immediately. And never, ever penalize your appointee for telling you you're wrong. He or she is doing it for your own good and at your request, remember? If you insist on killing the messenger, it won't take long before your staff refuses to point out that the emperor has no clothes. That means you're on your own . . . just when you are most in need of their help.

A critical part of forecasting involves determining the make-or-break factor. Every corporation has one . . . or it's in deep weeds. The make-or-break factor is the one thing so important to survival that if your corporation does it poorly, it doesn't matter what else it does well. You're dead. Conversely, if you get it right, it doesn't matter what else you do wrong. The trick is to find that factor and focus, focus, focus.

Since the make-or-break factor usually grows out of your corporation's internal and external environment, that's where to begin. Simply ask yourself five questions:

1. What are the five factors having the greatest positive effect on your corporation?
2. What are the five factors having the greatest negative effect?
3. Of these ten, which are most likely to be the make-or-break factors? Pick three and prioritize them.
4. For each one, to what extent can you predict its likelihood?
5. For each one, to what extent can you predict the corporation's response?

To evaluate the risk factor, review your answers in terms of Figure 10-1, which spells out the relationship between the degree of certainty that something will happen and the degree of certainty of the corporation's response.

Let's look at this process in terms of marketing. Whenever a company makes a strategic move, it incurs some degree of risk. Any corporation has only so much in the way of personnel, money, raw materials, and production and distribution capabilities. Strategy is simply the allocation of these resources—who gets what to accomplish a particular goal. In effect, the company is betting those resources on its marketing plan being right. The risk may also involve more than resources. There are opportunity costs: Those resources could be doing something else. There's also the risk of damage to the reputation of the company and to its products and services. (This can spill down into risk to your IS organization or department.)

To make sure that it's allocating resources correctly, the corporation should ask itself "What is our differential advantage?" What is it that separates your employer from others in the same industry? Strategy consists of finding a viable strategic advantage and then maximizing it.

This could have a crisis effect on IS—and provide it with a significant opportunity. I suspect that, for many companies in the 1990s, information will be the differential advantage. The emphasis will be on having the right information in the right

Figure 10-1. Evaluating risk in terms of the predictability of events and the corporate response to them.

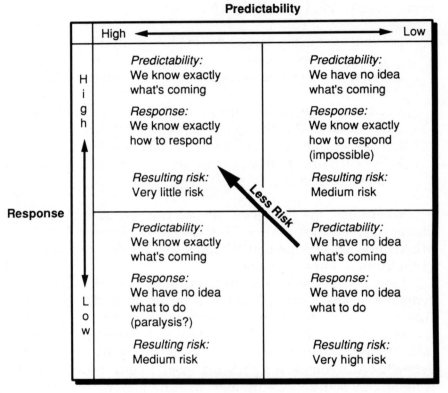

place at the right time. An IS organization that can position itself to provide the information that allows the corporation to react quickly and correctly to competitive events will be able to write its own ticket.

IS has a vested interest, both for its own good and that of the corporation, in getting involved in the strategic planning process with senior management. A curious fact about corporations is that the people in IS tend to be very bright. In school, they got A's and B's. And the CEOs they work for? They got C's. But they knew what they wanted. As James R. Barker, former chairman of what used to be Moore McCormack Resources (now owned by Southdown, Inc.), has pointed out: "Businesses aren't run by geniuses. It is a matter of putting one foot after another in a logical fashion. The trick is in knowing what direction you want to go."

Strategic planning can help a corporation get where it's going. But it's even more important in determining if that is indeed where it should be going. If a corporation is headed for the edge of a cliff, the last thing it needs is to get there more efficiently. Thus, planning always involves risk. The purpose of strategic management is to select those risks we want to take and then to manage them.

Chapter 11

Defining Your
Marketing Strategy

Management by objectives works if you know the objectives. Ninety percent of the time you don't.

—*Peter F. Drucker*

In previous chapters, I have laid the groundwork for your understanding of the value of marketing IS internally. First, I tried to convince you that marketing IS is critical to the success of the IS organization. Second, everything a corporation does—and by definition that means everything that the people who work for the corporation do—should evolve out of the corporation's overall strategic plan. I wanted you to start thinking strategically. Now that you're in that groove, I can talk marketing. Your company's marketing plan evolves from the corporate strategic plan. So should the IS organization's marketing plan, unless you wish to be remembered as the Wrong-way Corrigan of IS.

All marketing starts with market research. You must begin by studying the existing situation. Otherwise, how else will you know that you have improved it? Analyze your project operations (what IS does) and your project resources (what IS uses—people, dollars, equipment, supplies—to do them). Because these resources are finite, they are project restraints. What do your clients need (or think they need)? How does that square with the strategic plan? Finally, how can you allocate your resources so as to give your clients what they want (or need) in keeping with the demands of the strategic plan?

If this sounds a bit like systems analysis, there are similarities. A detailed checklist of what your market research should cover is included at the end of this chapter. When your research is complete, you will have the raw materials necessary to define the basic elements of your marketing strategy: target, focus, and impact factors.

These are the building blocks of your basic marketing strategy:

Target + Focus + Impact Factors = Strategy

Now let's look at the role that each of these elements plays in helping IS to determine its strategy.

IS Strategy

Target

All too often IS planners jump the gun and define technology in terms of specific hardware and/or software as the target of their marketing efforts. This approach rapidly turns into selling and, without appropriate marketing, clients become resistant and sometimes downright surly. And rightfully so.

As indicated in Figure 11-1, the target part of the equation is sequential. The technology is actually at the end of the target chain, not at the beginning.

Before we can target a specific technology as a solution, we must first address four issues: name/group recognition; working relationships; credibility; and product/service awareness. Only after we've dealt with these issues—and in this order—can we discuss technology.

Here's why. The object of our technology, as pointed out earlier, is not information but organizational relationships. If we target technology prematurely, we neglect our own organizational relationships. Instead, we get sidetracked—and sometimes sand-bagged—by having to deal with negative client responses:

Figure 11-1. The marketing target chain.

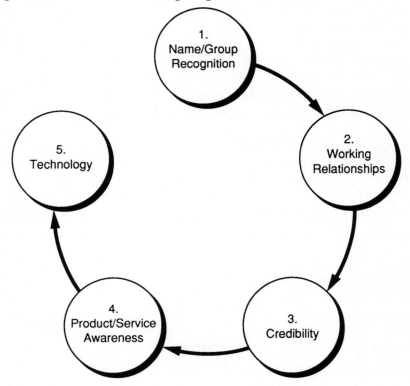

"So, who are you anyway?" (lack of name or group recog-
   nition)
"I've never worked with you before." (no working relation-
   ship established)
"Do you know what you are doing?" (lack of credibility)
"What do you do?" (lack of product or service awareness)

   There are tactics for working our way through the marketing
target chain. For now, suffice it to say that it is a strategic error
to target technology and bypass the preceding links in the chain.

Focus

We need at all times to be clear about the focus of our marketing
efforts. Figure 11-2, the Marketing Focus Wheel, is a clear reminder
of three different kinds of communication efforts:

Figure 11-2. The marketing focus wheel.

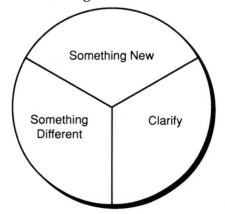

1. Are we trying to create awareness of or educate clients about something new (for example, a technology that's new, or at least new to the corporation)?

2. Are we merely promoting something different? (This is something that's not new, just a change. It could be as simple as changing the brand of floppies you buy, or as complex as changing mainframe systems.)

3. Is our intent to clarify because we suspect our clients are confused or misinformed? (Explaining issues of incompatibility to clients, for example, often reduces IPPs to shouting "Because! That's why!")

Once we have pinpointed the focus of our marketing effort, we can ask ourselves the following questions, projecting different responses based on what our focus is:

- *"Who is the audience and what do I know about them?"* For example, if your marketing focus is on something new and your audience is middle managers, you know that their ears will be tuned to day-by-day operations and operating costs.
- *"What does the audience want/need to hear?"* If your marketing focus is on something different and your audience is staff level, they will want to know if they are going to have to give up something they are comfortable with. If you are marketing the

need for a new voice message system to replace answering machines, they will be listening for hands-on benefits and ease of use. Senior management will be more interested in knowing why the current system is inadequate and what the justification for the investment in something different is. In one corporation, IS wanted to make a significant change in the configuration of some new, and very expensive, technology, the purchase of which had been previously approved by the board of directors. The head of IS prepared an elaborate fifteen-minute presentation, using printed and bound handouts and four-color, schematic overhead transparencies to explain the proposed change at the next board meeting. Two minutes into his presentation—and before he could use a single transparency—the IS executive was interrupted by the vice chairman, who said, "Let me get this straight. If we approve this change, we'll get more capacity and save $600,000? Done. Next item on the agenda. . . ."

- *"Why might the audience resist our marketing efforts?"* How can you adjust your marketing effort to minimize resistance? Suppose your marketing focus is on clarifying because your clients are constantly asking you to do application development, which is not part of your mission. You can anticipate your clients being less than thrilled with your "Sorry, Charlie" message. You know they will then ask, "If you can't help us, who can?" Your response of "I don't know" or "No one" will not be endearing. Instead, why not try to facilitate an agreement for your clients' management to discuss this need with the IS management? Even though this time you can't help your clients directly, playing a role in pointing them in the direction of a solution strengthens your position as a marketer.

- *What can our marketing efforts do for this audience or to them?* (That's a subtle but important distinction.)

Impact Factors

Once target and focus have been identified, the marketing impact factors, as shown in Figure 11-3, remain to be considered. No matter what you end up with for target and focus, you must still evaluate the following:

Figure 11-3. Marketing impact factors.

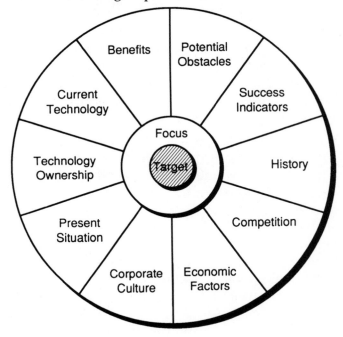

- *Benefits.* It's the nature of the beast to want to know "What's in it for me?" People are more apt to tolerate some initial confusion and disruption if they know there will be a payoff for them downstream. Solid marketing strategies acknowledge and address both positive and negative impacts up front. It's especially important to cover the negative effects. People don't like surprises. They're usually unpleasant. If the negatives surface later, your clients are likely to think you hustled them. If, instead, you level with them about the downside of your proposal, they are much more likely to accept the positive side.

- *Potential obstacles.* The target and focus analyses can help you anticipate many potential obstacles. If your IS management has asked you to promote the benefits of networking PCs (something new), you can anticipate resistance from the financial analysts who currently use and control their spreadsheets in a stand-alone mode. The success of your IS marketing effort in this instance depends upon your being able to reassure the financial analysts that the security and integrity of their data will be preserved in a networked environment.

- *Success indicators.* How will you know if your marketing efforts are successful? In addition to some of the indicators discussed in Chapter 4, others might include your audience's requesting additional information if you focused on something new or something different, or your clients' adhering to the points made if you had focused on clarifying.

- *Corporate culture.* This is a combination of the corporation's reward/punishment system (every human institution has one) and custom ("the way we do things around here"). People who ignore corporate culture are known as ex-employees. If your company makes it clear that it doesn't like people who rock the boat, would you really want to target a new, high-risk technology? Conversely, a "play-it-safe" proposal might get nuked in a high-risk environment, the kind found in some aggressive consumer products companies, some Silicon Valley companies, and some financial organizations (at least up until the October 1987 market crash and the S&L crisis). In this sort of "rock-n-roll" corporate climate, people who stay in the middle of the road tend to get run over. In any case, never, never ignore your corporate culture because it defines the parameters of the possible.

Other cultural items include:

- *Any history affecting the marketing effort.*
- *Any competition, external or internal.*
- *Economic factors such as budgets.* Again, all those high-priced microchip toys have to be paid for in real dollars. And because the resource pie is finite, any dollars earmarked for IS can be diverted to you only by subtracting them from someone else's budget.
- *Analysis of the present situation.*
- *Project ownership.* Once you hand it over, it's not your system any more.
- *The status of current technology systems.*

Strategy

Careful consideration and analysis of the target, focus, and impact factors form the foundation of a marketing strategy to help ensure that the necessary awareness and education precede technology decisions. The strategy itself defines what needs to be addressed. Detail the tactics to be used in defining how to implement the strategy.

Let's go back to our example of marketing the need for a new voice message system to replace answering machines. Suppose that, for whatever internal reason, a corporate decision has come down from on high that facsimile will be the technology of choice and the cost of its purchase and maintenance will be assumed by the field offices. Since we're now pursuing a different goal, both a different marketing objective and a different strategy will—or should—result.

The new objective might be: "Helping field office management to understand the decision to implement facsimile in all field offices." The resulting strategy would be geared to management and would focus on comparisons of the technologies considered, including factors such as cost and how these technologies fit in with the corporation's longer-term business plans.

In either case, once the specific marketing objective has been defined and narrowed, and the target, focus, and impact factors have been outlined, the strategy will become apparent. In short, the strategy defines the *what*, while the tactics help define *how* to implement the strategy.

Conducting Your Marketing Approach

The first thing you have to consider when undertaking a market research program is cost. You should concentrate on increasing the value of IS while maintaining or utilizing the resources you already have in place.

Most of the marketing skills outlined here are in fact designed to enable you to market IS *without having to increase your resources*. In most cases, you can effectively market the value of IS without either hiring more people or paying a high fee to a consulting or marketing firm from Wall Street or Madison Avenue.

In the various steps of the program that follow, I'll suggest always that you use inexpensive methods to reach your audience. For example, you can create newsletters on existing word processors, or generate graphics via desk-top publishing software.

In a general sense, however, you need to have answers for questions about cost, especially since marketing for IS represents an added departmental endeavor. For instance, how are you going to answer this one? "How can you guys think about increasing your cost? You're already a burden."

Think about it this way. If you follow the steps presented here, if you instill an excitement for marketing in your staff, and a respect for IS in the minds of your business colleagues, then the investment of time, effort, and material will not be evident— or it will be passed over as a judicious use of overhead personnel.

There is, after all, a cost involved in anything having to do with a business. There's a cost involved when you turn the lights on. There's a cost involved when someone empties the waste baskets. There's a cost involved when two people converse— whether it concerns a business problem or last night's baseball scores. There's a cost involved whenever an employee sits and thinks about something unrelated to business—like what color to paint the house when vacation rolls around.

Involved in your IS marketing plan will be the time and effort for such things as meetings and the forming and structuring of committees, some time required of your business clients, some minimum material costs, and some miscellaneous services from other internal departments. The point is, these are existing resources. You are not asking anyone to pile up a huge debt or to blow a budget by hiring outside agencies.

Yes, there is a cost involved in anything, but it's all relative. This is a situation in which the ideal challenges the reality. In a cost system that charges 100 percent of a service department back to an on-line department, the assumption is that eight hours per day per person are accountable. This is the ideal. The reality is that the time spent discussing baseball scores or thinking about painting a house is not considered. We're not talking, after all, about a production worker whose contribution to corporate profits can be accurately measured by the actual work accomplished in this same eight-hour day.

Salaried people's efforts are measured in terms of attitude and departmental, or company, success. Neither the latest IS technology nor the rigid control arms of Big Brother can measure the dedication of the human brain.

Inspiration is the proven catalyst for positive human reaction. The aim, therefore, is to inspire, and in these pages I hope to give you the tools you need.

There are basically three types of marketing:

1. *Mass marketing*. This is a shotgun approach. It targets everybody as an audience.
2. *Indiscriminate marketing*. Here, there is no specific plan. It's just "Throw it out there and see what happens," or, as they say on Madison Avenue, "Run up the flag and see who salutes!"
3. *Target marketing*. This aims at specific audiences and special requirements that need to be filled. Let your research include consideration of these issues and the targeted audience.

Under these general headings there are two basic strategies that apply: positive and negative marketing. Positive, in the case of IS, would mean striving for a positive reaction from your audience, aiming for a positive appreciation of you and your technology.

Negative marketing, now much in vogue in consumer types of advertising and marketing, involves trying to reverse an opinion already established. Popular TV campaigns use this strategy. Think of the Pepsi-Cola/Coca-Cola wars; Chrysler versus the Japanese; and the downright mudslinging of political advertising.

I strongly recommend the positive approach for you in your research and planning. But be aware of the negative, as wayward thinking often leads to the negative.

Also beware of the "Halo Effect"! Not you, of course, but there are others whose marketing plans have gone astray because their egos produced a saintly halo that clouded their vision. They were so great, they thought, that they lost track of the plan's initial goal. It's difficult to see clearly when the halo is right in front of your eyes.

Now, here is a checklist of the steps involved in researching your marketing approach:

☐ *Identify your primary objectives.* What is it that you're trying to do? Count the steps you're going to take. Identify and measure the potential value of the products and services you're trying to market. A rule of thumb might be to look for products or services that can be highly leveraged without expanding capabilities and with only minimum training.

☐ *Review for the proper fit.* Does what you're trying to market fit comfortably into the regular business organization? For extended use, your marketing effort should be closely linked to business possibilities.

☐ *Talk to clients about their perception of your service.* Lay it on the table: Ask them what they think of your plan and your ability to carry it out. Their perception of you is important, and a "pre-game" dialogue will make them feel a part of the project.

☐ *Identify your support service requirements.* List the support services that will be required by your plan—full-time, part-time, vendors perhaps (both the internal and external possibilities). Consider the staff time, the client base, all the elements that you will have to support on an ongoing basis to pull it off. Don't get trapped into thinking that because marketing may give you more clients you'll automatically need more staff. Remember that marketing is dynamic, an ongoing activity, so look carefully at the support you will need to maintain this ongoing activity.

☐ *Identify current clients who are using technology.* Look for internal technology competition or outside vendors or services that could affect the execution of your plan. Be aware!

☐ *Research the pricing factors.* Analyze your requirements from the cost point of view. Be prepared! Consider the product or service involved. For example, the cost of putting on a demo or a "technology fair," getting the equipment in place, laying the cabling, or building the booth are all extra cost factors. They may be well worth the money in your opinion, but be prepared with numbers to support your plan. Separate the extras from the fixed costs and build them into your plan.

☐ *Build a strategy for handling negative perception.* Put your knowledge of corporate partners into play. Anticipate a negative response from the usual suspects and build an answer to this probable confrontation into your plan. Identify the resistance at the outset.

☐ *Identify the controlling issues.* Consider the standards, the documentation, the security, and the technical constraints that you may have to face. These elements could well determine the direction you take. For example, an identifying logo for your IS plan might conflict with company policy regarding the use of anything but the company logo. Double-check the security issues and your own technical ability to pull it off.

☐ *Forecast the length of your plan's effectiveness.* Marketing is dynamic, an ongoing thrust, but you need to upgrade it continually. Even very familiar products, like Coca-Cola, change their look from time to time—subtly perhaps, but it's done. The reason is that interest must be regenerated before enthusiasm wanes. Be reasonable in your estimate of the effective life of your plan.

☐ *Forecast the expected shifts in demand.* Things change! That includes technology, individual job descriptions, corporate images, even management philosophy (for instance, phases such as "management by objective" or "managing for excellence"). Consider the possibility of change in your research, and build some flexibility to cope with it into your plan.

☐ *Look for possible barriers to your success.* Politics, for example, is not necessarily a negative consideration, but you must recognize it as a factor and research the potential areas where it could develop. Your own IS staff could present some barriers if there is misunderstanding, job insecurity, or just plain professional objection in your camp. Client support is always vital. You must have support, so try to anticipate the corporate areas where your supporters could lose their enthusiasm, and aim your communication there. Also, be aware of vendors. As we know, there are even leaks in the White House, and if vendors get a sniff of what you're doing they could possibly compete and destroy.

With your research checklist in hand and your strategy developed, it's time now to prepare your plan.

Chapter 12

Preparing Your IS Marketing Plan

Good results without good planning come from good luck, not good management.

—David Jaquith, President, Vega Industries, Inc.

You have finally arrived. You've contemplated the concepts and issues. You've done your market research. You've thought through your strategy. Now it happens: It's time for you to prepare the marketing plan for your IS organization.

To help you assess your best potential marketing area, narrow down the alternatives, and turn thought into action, use the marketing action funnel illustrated in Figure 12-1.

The marketing action funnel allows you to choose from among everything you could do only the most important tasks you will in fact do. If you apply it correctly, the funnel inevitably leads you to those tasks that offer IS the greatest return on its efforts.

Let's assume that you have utilized the marketing action funnel and have identified your target area and what it is you want to market.

Developing an effective marketing plan requires thirteen simple steps. Let me walk you through the steps so that you can clearly understand the purpose and value of each. (A sample use

Figure 12-1. The marketing action funnel.

of these steps can be seen in Chapter 18, in the Sleepy Valley Vineyards case study.)

 1. *Set objectives and goals.* This is where you clearly identify the objectives and goals of your potential marketing plan, such as to introduce a new technology to the executives of your company or to improve the tarnished image of your department.

 2. *Establish a measurable outcome.* This outcome will indicate the success of your marketing plan. Here are a few examples: receiving buy-in from clients, being invited to a client's business planning sessions, or gaining client commitment.

 3. *Prepare your audience profile.* Who is your target audience? You need to locate your audience within appropriate categories. Identify who they are, their specific needs, work environment, strengths, weaknesses, average age, income, sex, departmental location, or any other factors that could affect your plan. Remem-

ber that each audience has its own special needs. What do you want them to do, not do, or let you do? What do they have to know to do it? By when do they have to know it for the desired action (or inaction) to happen?

4 & 5. *Identify positive/resistive forces*. Generate a complete list of the issues that affect your audience's attitude toward IS. Does IS have a poor image? Does IS have a good track record with this kind of technology? Does IS have a good relationship with the target audience? Is the affected audience resistant to new technology? Do you have positive relationships in these areas? Identify as many issues as you can before reviewing for the primary obstacles and support. Then build a strategy that addresses the negatives and utilizes the positives in the development of your plan in Step 10.

6. *Focus on primary concerns*. These are concerns that you must address if you are to be successful with your marketing plan. Items to consider would include money, time, resources, the competition, vendors, culture, sponsors, lobbyists, and stakeholders. Write them all down, evaluate them, then prioritize.

7. *Decide on your approach*. What approach will your marketing plan use? Should it be a hard approach—aggressive, bottom-line-oriented, quick to a closure? Or should you use a soft approach—emphasizing the long term, seed planting, slower intentional results?

8. *Choose a theme*. Your theme represents you and your efforts, saying in effect, "This is who we are, this is what we are trying to do." A slogan such as "Bring on the Competition" may address the issue of IS becoming a profit center, for example.

9. *Find partners*. Identify people within your organization who can help your marketing efforts: a sponsor, a lobbyist, a stakeholder.

10. *Design your marketing plan*. This is the most crucial point. This is where you decide what your tactical plan will consist of: who, what, when, where, and how you will implement it.

The remaining steps 11–13 will be discussed later in this chapter. Before finishing step 10, the marketing plan, you need to complete a shelf plan. A shelf plan is a first cut, beginning to end, of your marketing plan. Doing a rough shelf plan before you plan individual marketing efforts in detail offers a number of advantages:

- The shelf plan keeps you focused on the big picture.
- The shelf plan helps you to avoid the trap of putting a lot of time into planning the first few steps and then rushing through the last steps as you approach the deadline. Often IS managers get too bogged down too early in the process. Spending 90 percent of their time on the first few steps, they then go into general hysteria to complete the remaining 90 percent of the work in 10 percent of the time. Sound familiar?
- The shelf plan gives you a "rough cut" plan on the shelf that's ready to go. Should you come down with the flu two weeks before your deadline, your team still has a plan it can go with.

Here are some pointers on creating your shelf plan:

- *List specific content topics.* Brainstorm a more-than-complete list of topics. Discourage negative comments at this stage and don't permit anyone to shoot down any idea, no matter how bizarre it may seem. The purpose here is to loosen up the mind so that it can make as many connections as possible and generate a veritable core dump of suggestions. The more ideas you come up with—the good, the bad, and the ugly—at this brainstorming stage, the more usable ideas you will end up with. So list all the possibilities that may fit within your content parameters. Be creative, even off-the-wall. You'll have time later to pare down the list.
- *Identify time frames.* Have you allotted a realistic amount of time for getting your shelf plan in order? If not, how much time do you need? In this connection, consider:

  - The amount of time away from the job necessary to create the shelf plan.

- Absorption time, or the amount of material that a hypothetical audience can digest at one time.
- Practice time for your team. For example, don't ever make a presentation without rehearsing it first. Rehearsal time is the key to reaching your audience.

■ *Build the shelf plan.* Sort and sequence the topics you have come up with and be sure to include a variety of techniques and activities with which to hook your audience. Provide for smooth transitions between topics. And remember, people have a limited endurance for too much of anything. For instance, a presentation that is all lecture or all slides or all demonstration becomes acutely boring. Break it up. Spice it up with some fun and games, hands-on opportunities, colorful graphics, and perhaps a promotional guide.

■ *Debug the shelf plan.* Now's the time to review what you've got and to modify the plan by removing whatever doesn't work, whatever seems confused, or whatever is redundant. Ask yourself:

- Does the marketing sequence work?
- Are any topics missing? Or covered twice?
- Are the assigned time frames appropriate?
- Are the rhythm and pace of the marketing program right?
- Are review and feedback opportunities built in?
- Does the whole thing make sense?

■ *Plan in detail the material elements of your event.* Be sure that the location/environment you have chosen for your event will support the nature and goals of your program. For example, if you're doing a lengthy presentation with demonstrations, make sure that the chairs are comfortable. If you have handouts, make sure that the lighting is adequate so people can read without eyestrain. Research the noise level of the room and make sure that the temperature won't send your audience to sleep.

Sound pretty obvious? Perhaps. But more than one presentation has been shot down by an uncomfortable audience whose needs were ignored by the presenters. One CEO who was too vain to wear his glasses in public often had trouble reading print and audiovisual materials. Department heads who picked up on this used the largest type possible for their proposals, which tended to sail through. Department heads who missed this signal usually found themselves pinned down in the middle of a budgetary free-fire zone.

Now that you have an understanding of the development of a shelf plan through step 10, let's continue with steps 11–13 of your IS marketing plan:

11. *Review your plan.* Put the plan on the shelf for a short period and forget about it. Then go back and review the plan for final adjustments. Upon returning, you will be able to view the plan with a fresh eye and to evaluate it with much more objectivity. Show it no mercy. Ask someone who may not respond to it positively to critique it. Flush out as much as you can and refine, refine, refine.

12. *Execute it.* This is the moment of truth. Look on it as a one-shot trial in which you're testing a new systems program and daring it to fail. It's no time for half-hearted measures. Give it your best shot with your best talent. (You may want to have a pilot program of some kind first, if possible.)

13. *Evaluate it.* This is postmortem time in which you check out the success or lack of success of your efforts. Did you meet your objectives? Are you now receiving fewer complaint calls? Are you more professionally recognized? Did you gain the extra funding you need?

Now that the thirteen steps have been explained, they are concisely presented in Figure 12-2. Each step's purpose is summarized for your easy reference.

Goals of Evaluating Your Marketing Plan

Let's look at the evaluation of your marketing plan in more detail. This step is crucial. By considering to what degree your plan worked, you will learn valuable lessons on preparing future plans.

Figure 12-2. Thirteen steps to developing your IS marketing plan.

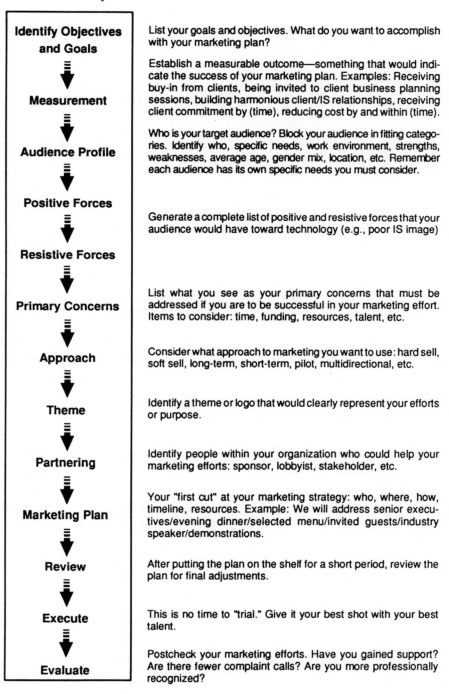

Identify Objectives and Goals	List your goals and objectives. What do you want to accomplish with your marketing plan?
Measurement	Establish a measurable outcome—something that would indicate the success of your marketing plan. Examples: Receiving buy-in from clients, being invited to client business planning sessions, building harmonious client/IS relationships, receiving client commitment by (time), reducing cost by and within (time).
Audience Profile	Who is your target audience? Block your audience in fitting categories. Identify who, specific needs, work environment, strengths, weaknesses, average age, gender mix, location, etc. Remember each audience has its own specific needs you must consider.
Positive Forces	
Resistive Forces	Generate a complete list of positive and resistive forces that your audience would have toward technology (e.g., poor IS image)
Primary Concerns	List what you see as your primary concerns that must be addressed if you are to be successful in your marketing effort. Items to consider: time, funding, resources, talent, etc.
Approach	Consider what approach to marketing you want to use: hard sell, soft sell, long-term, short-term, pilot, multidirectional, etc.
Theme	Identify a theme or logo that would clearly represent your efforts or purpose.
Partnering	Identify people within your organization who could help your marketing efforts: sponsor, lobbyist, stakeholder, etc.
Marketing Plan	Your "first cut" at your marketing strategy: who, where, how, timeline, resources. Example: We will address senior executives/evening dinner/selected menu/invited guests/industry speaker/demonstrations.
Review	After putting the plan on the shelf for a short period, review the plan for final adjustments.
Execute	This is no time to "trial." Give it your best shot with your best talent.
Evaluate	Postcheck your marketing efforts. Have you gained support? Are there fewer complaint calls? Are you more professionally recognized?

Source: Ouellette & Associates Consulting, Inc.

Evaluate the following areas and objectives; ask yourself in each case whether the goal was met, or how close you came:

- *Content*. Content should have measured up to audience expectations and the message clearly understood.
- *Delivery*. Delivery should have been well paced, neither too fast nor too slow. A proper delivery technique should have been utilized.
- *Media and technology*. The media and technology selected should have been appropriate to the audience and the topic.
- *Staff*. Staff members should have been thoroughly prepared. They should have received proper training skills and achieved the right level of sophistication.
- *Demonstration of the impact of IS on the corporation*. You should have been able to strengthen the link between IS and the corporation's business results by providing quantitative measures of the value of IS. Equally important, you should evaluate whether you overcame any of the barriers that have prevented other parts of the organization from understanding and accepting the practical results of your services.

Suggested Evaluation Processes

Two possibilities for feedback are questionnaires and interviews. Interviews are more flexible than questionnaires, but are also more time-consuming.

You must also decide when the evaluation should take place. It could occur during the promotional event, immediately following it, or as follow-up checking afterward.

As a result of your analysis, you should be able to answer the following:

- Do we need to add, change, or delete content?
- Does our delivery need adjustment?
- Do our marketing materials need refinement?
- Do we need to improve upon our message by strengthening our links with business performance?

You may wish to build a database to keep track of what has worked and what hasn't. You can keep a general track record and include trends to keep up-to-date.

Summary

Is all this a lot of work? Of course. Even the best of plans often degenerates into hard work. Is it worth it? You better believe it. An effective marketing plan for your IS organization will:

- Serve as a road map to where you want to go.
- Allocate projects, responsibilities, and deadlines.
- Educate people involved in the plan of their responsibilities.
- Obtain resources for allocation and implementation.
- Make better use of those resources.
- Stimulate your organization's best thinking.
- Improve your management control and strategy implementation.
- Trigger awareness of problems, threats, and opportunities.
- Create an awareness of the true value of IS.

In short, a good marketing plan is more than just a work tool for the IS organization. It is above all a survival tool.

Although a presentation format is often assumed for a typical marketing plan and has been used as an example here, realize that your plan may include a variety of methods to achieve your goals. You could plan a luncheon, dinner, technology fair, outing, special guest speaker, and so on. There are virtually no limits.

Remember nothing was presented in this chapter that you can't do or master. The thirteen steps have been proven effective time and time again. Some organizations have changed the sequence of the steps. It made it easier for them. That's okay, but make sure you do each step and recognize its purpose. One step not properly executed may lead to the failure of your marketing plan. In most cases, you will have a one-shot chance at that particular marketing plan, so take it slowly and seriously.

Chapter 13

Evaluating Your Target Audience

Who are those guys?
—Butch Cassidy

There go my people. I am their leader. I must catch up with them.
—Mahatma Gandhi

Behind almost every bad organizational move is a decision made in a vacuum. Usually it's a case of the decision makers not having the slightest idea of how the people affected by their decision will react. This happens when the decision makers just assume that they know (or know better) what people want. Then, when those affected—customers, clients, staff, the public—vent their rage, the people at the switch scratch their heads, befuddled and unsure where they went wrong.

Those people with the bewildered looks on their faces never bothered to study the affected groups. They never did an audience profile. The essence of this audience research is pretty simple:

- Find out what your audience wants. Give it to them.
- Find out what your audience hates. Stop it.

Slick, huh? Actually, it's more complex than that—but not much more. The IS exec is not marketing technology. He or she is marketing solutions. Since you can't have a solution without first having a problem—and someone who's the proud owner of that problem—helping that person entails a five-phase process:

1. Profile the clients.
2. Contract with your clients. Make a commitment to helping them.
3. Study and understand their needs.
4. Evaluate alternatives.
5. Match the solution to their needs.

Because the end product of information technology changes IS relationships, our process must always begin and end with the client. For IS, I have defined our clients as five different audiences:

1. CEO/senior executive staff
2. Senior management
3. Middle management
4. Clients in general
5. IS staff

Each group has its own needs and its own concerns. Ignoring the differences between them is like trying to put a $5\frac{1}{4}''$ floppy into a $3\frac{1}{2}''$ drive. What are the concerns of each group? Let's take a look at some of the known audience concerns that you must address if your marketing plan is to succeed.

Primary Client Concerns by Organizational Placement

Figure 13-1 represents your basic organizational pyramid. In the spirit of equal opportunity, let's reverse that order now. What do people really want? Knowing this will help you to create a much stronger and effective marketing plan. For example, if I use the word "profit," CEOs would probably state, "Great, our shareholders and board of directors will be happy." Senior management upon hearing "profit" may reply, "Great, we have done our job, let's refine the organization to ensure a profit next

Figure 13-1. Segmenting your internal audiences.

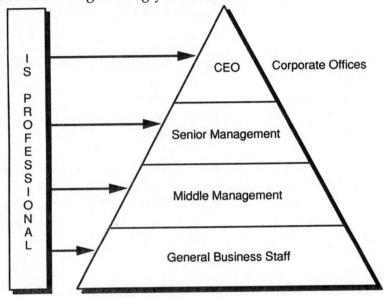

year." Middle management upon hearing "profit" may say, "Great, we can apply for a bigger budget or add staff." While the general business staff upon hearing "profit" may well ask, "Where's our raise?" Same word but very different meaning as you work within the corporation. This is why it is important to understand your audience concerns by organizational placement.

Clients in General

Clients' concerns center around the following:

- *Recognition.* This is the primary need. Most people want to be recognized and respected for their contributions.
- *Job security. The Desk Set* was the 1957 Spencer Tracy/Katharine Hepburn movie that asked, "Will I still have a job after you bring in your computer?" A third of a century later, this is still a burning question for many employees. They've seen too many "computer casualties" to blindly accept IS's assurances that technology will simply make their jobs more fulfilling. That promise ranks right up there with "the check's in the mail."

- *Income and benefits.*

- *Self-actualization and other good stuff.* This is decidedly last. No amount of job satisfaction or psychological fulfillment is meaningful to people who still feel unappreciated and are worried where their next paycheck will be coming from.

Middle Management

These are the nose-to-the-grindstone people. Their concerns are quite pragmatic:

- Effects on the budget
- Benefits to the department
- Time involved
- Training requirements
- Additional staff requirements
- Effects on manager's staff/job classification
- Effects on manager's degree of control
- Effects on current work flow
- Need for minimal technical talk

Senior Management

Most junior executives or staff people are somewhat fearful when dealing with senior management. I find this sad. Oh, they can be demanding, to be sure. But, from my experience, they are the easiest group to work with. Typically, they listen to business logic and then make their decisions. What more do you want?

Although you must be prepared and respect the time allocated to you, you probably will not find a more supportive audience. They are a group we need to focus on and with whom we must go beyond trend analysis and forecasting types of applications. One CEO I spoke with recently stated that his biggest problem with IS and technology was not executives' fear of usage or willingness to learn but rather IS's inability to provide relational application access to them (that is, having a system that is tied into several other systems). In other words, as he stated, "IS just doesn't understand our needs at this level of the corporation." We need to understand the true meaning of that statement.

When planning a marketing program aimed at high-level executives, you may want to consider the following executive concerns:

- Executive time constraints
- Corporate implications
- Human resources requirements
- Costs
- Commitments required
- Implementation schedule
- Benefits (not only monetary)
- Dislike of technical talk (whether industry jargon or IS buzz words)
- Appreciation of the direct approach

The IS Staff

It would be a mistake to ignore your IS colleagues as a target audience. Don't assume that because they are IS people they will automatically be behind every IS program. They too are affected by marketing programs and will exhibit some of the same concerns that any other employee has plus some that are specific to IS. Here are some concerns you need to consider:

- Impact on the jobs in IS
- What the benefits are to the department
- Impact on your clients
- The timetable of activities
- Impact on current operations and applications
- Qualifications of your staff
- Standards and procedures
- Learning to do without technical jargon

Now that we have looked at potential audience concerns, it is time to find out how we can identify the areas we want to reach.

Figure 13-2.   The client map.

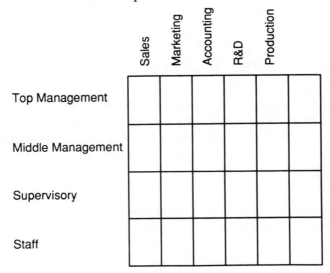

The Client Map

To help you focus more clearly on which audience you want to address first, I provide you with an approach I call the client map, illustrated in Figure 13-2.

First, draw a grid on a flip chart or large sheet of paper. The columns of the grid will represent the departments or groups within the organization—such functional areas as sales, marketing, operations, R&D, and accounting. The rows represent the levels within the organizational hierarchy (limited for the purposes of simplicity to just four levels: top management, middle management, supervisory, and staff).

The second stage of this client mapping exercise is to assign the groups a priority based upon their impact on the success of the organization as a whole. Then list the key business goals of each of these groups, identify the key players in each, and select the top priorities to evaluate as marketing targets. Develop a plan to communicate to these people the services that the IS department has to offer and the benefits of using them. This exercise should be repeated at least once a year. In addition, the client map should be saved to evaluate progress against last year's map.

You should also place a date indicating the last time you or your IS organization was in front of or made a pitch to this group.

Obstacles to Effective Marketing

There's really only one obstacle—people. As discussed earlier, the path to the successful implementation of new technology is strewn with resistance and fear . . . and with the bodies of IPPs who ignored these factors. Most of this resistance can be traced to four sources:

1. *Lack of IS education.* People may not have the educational background to understand what the technology can do or even to be able to use it.

2. *An inappropriate reward structure.* Charlie puts in a lot of overtime hours. The time-and-a-half makes a significant difference in how his family lives. You walk in and explain to him that, thanks to computerization, he will no longer be burdened by all that awful overtime. What kind of a reaction do you think you're going to get? Salaried employees may like eliminating those extra hours without pay. But cut out an hourly worker's overtime and you may be wiping out his kids' school money or Christmas. Perhaps that's an unavoidable side effect of a change the corporation has to make. However, don't expect rose petals strewn at your feet if moving away from the current structure penalizes people for accepting your technology. And these penalties need not be solely financial.

3. *Effect on power and control.* Computerizing the sales and customer service function will allow the company to halve the size of that department and cut costs by 40 percent. You expect the people whose jobs will be eliminated to hate you. But when an infuriated head of that department trashes you for "trying to screw up my operation," you're surprised. Don't be. That person may have a strong sense of loyalty to those of her people who will be released. Moreover, in many companies, status and clout are measured by the size of your budget. You may be wiping out a good chunk of the manager's standing with her peers and boss.

And by the way, the people in charge of inventory may not approve of you either. Because the customer service terminals interface directly with the computerized inventory, they've lost some control over their area. They may not be amused.

4. *Complacency.* In one episode of the sitcom "Barney Miller," Lt. Harris bemoans the fact that he missed out on the chance to "get in on the ground floor" of Xerox when the stock was new and the price low. Why did he throw away this golden opportunity? "I couldn't see why anyone would want a machine when we had all this carbon paper." That was fiction but it happens in real life, too. Remember the manufacturers of mechanical calculators who chose to ignore electronic calculator technology when it first nosed over the horizon? A certain percentage of the human race simply believes that its market share was decreed by the Almighty. The dinosaurs thought their world wouldn't change either.

Force Field Analysis

To overcome these obstacles, the IS exec needs an organized plan of attack. One of the most effective tools I can offer to help organize this campaign is called force field analysis, illustrated in Figure 13-3.

Begin by identifying all the forces—both positive and negative—that relate to the acceptance of your marketing effort. The horizontal axis of the force field indicates the status quo. Beneath that line, list all the positive forces that are trying to push that line up. Above the axis, list all the negative factors that are trying to push that line down.

The next step is to pair off negatives with compensating positives. Ask yourself, or your staff, which positive will offset which negative. When you find a negative that doesn't have a positive to neutralize it, that's the problem to focus your efforts on. Don't try to blow the axis off the chart. Instead, realistically ask yourself how much of an improvement would eliminating that negative represent. Try for a reasonable percentage of upward movement.

Force field analysis can also be a highly useful tool in defusing emotional issues. Confrontations can sometimes be avoided sim-

Figure 13-3.   Force field analysis of positive and negative factors.

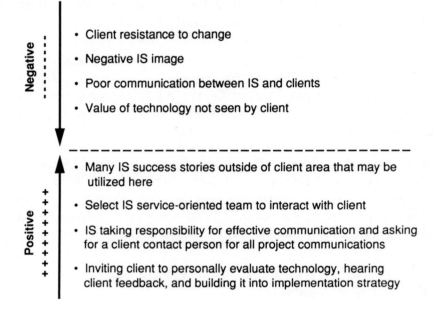

- Client resistance to change
- Negative IS image
- Poor communication between IS and clients
- Value of technology not seen by client

- Many IS success stories outside of client area that may be utilized here
- Select IS service-oriented team to interact with client
- IS taking responsibility for effective communication and asking for a client contact person for all project communications
- Inviting client to personally evaluate technology, hearing client feedback, and building it into implementation strategy

ply by listing the pros and cons on the chart. Just getting them on paper somehow makes the problem more objective and less personal. When people stare at the problem on paper (or flip chart or blackboard), they become more reasonable.

Overcoming Resistance and Fear

You now understand your audiences. You know who needs to be approached. You even know where the land mines—the forces of resistance and fear—are. The tricky part is avoiding them. It can be done. There are concrete steps you can take to overcome resistance and minimize fear. Don't expect a 100 percent conversion rate. Only dictatorships have unanimous elections, and lately even they can't get those kinds of numbers. But don't be discouraged. Progress can take many forms.

Increase awareness and understanding:

- Clearly convey the benefits of technology to your clients.

- Recognize that your client may lack knowledge of your services and technology (or anybody's technology).
- Plan ahead. Allow "absorption" time.
- Establish an ongoing communications procedure . . . and keep such channels open.

Provide incentives for use:

- Make the technology acceptable to the client's or user's peers.
- Escalate to include senior management. Corporate culture begins at the top. Seeing that the honchos are behind the technology and, where applicable, using it themselves will go a long way toward motivating others.
- Include incentives in the objectives.
- Provide public praise for clients who use your technology. Everyone wants to wear a white hat.

Maximize client control and decision making:

- Get your clients to participate in project and planning teams.
- Keep your clients informed and ask for feedback throughout the process.
- Provide additional functions and responsibilities.
- Have clients lead projects. They are much more likely to push for your program when it is their program.
- Be sensitive to power and control issues. Never blindly assume that anyone will give up budget, staff, power, status, or control without a fight.
- Plan for and execute systems handoffs. By vesting "ownership" of the systems in the hands of your clients, you create not only a powerful ally but also a system that will function more effectively. This can happen even when the manuals you give them read as if they had been written in Albanian.
- Provide layman-friendly manuals. With all due respect, technical writing is unintelligible to most people. If you want manuals that your clients can comprehend and use, go to your corporation's marketing writers or hire a free-

lance writer. But make sure that he or she is a quality writer who doesn't understand the technology you are implementing. Keep explaining it in one-syllable words until the writer grasps it and then let that person write it up that way. This process will frustrate you and offend your technical writers, but it will spare you the necessity of answering the same questions over and over again. If it's in the manual and in English, you may even end up with a happy client.

Generate enthusiasm and display personal confidence: If you come across as unsure whether or not your proposal is a good idea, your audience will probably agree with you. If IS is truly to become a service organization and become effective at marketing, department members must believe in the following Ten Commandments for long-term success:

1. Our clients are our purpose.
2. We need our clients' business.
3. Our clients are not changing our systems; they are enhancing them.
4. Serving our clients is not a favor we offer; it is mandatory.
5. Satisfying client business needs through technology is our only business.
6. Our clients are real people, not some imaginary stereotype we have created.
7. We don't argue with clients; we influence them.
8. Our clients have the requirements; we fulfill them.
9. Our clients deserve a professional attitude at all times.
10. Our clients are the conduit between us and the corporation we serve.

The Client Connection

This is another true story.

Once upon a time there was a department in a large organization. The staff of that department shared a large, common work area, the temperature of which was controlled by a single thermostat. The staff, which obviously didn't have enough to do, spent most of its time arguing about the temperature of the office area.

Periodically, someone from the "It's Too Hot" faction would march over to the west wall in a huff and turn the thermostat down. A minute and a huff later, a representative of the "It's Too Cold" faction would dramatically wrap her sweater around her, shiver her way to the thermostat, and turn it up. And so it went month after month. Not a particularly efficient use of energy—mechanical or human—but at least each side could take grim satisfaction in the fact that their opponents weren't comfortable either.

Enter The Solution. One Friday after working hours, a mainte-nance man, weary of it all, detached the wires that connected the disputed thermostat to the heating/air conditioning system and remounted the thermostat on the wall. On Monday morning, the hot/cold War resumed in earnest. Champions of each faction tried their hand at the thermostat. As usual, its setting was moved up and down at least a score of times a day. Only now, the temperature never changed. Nothing happened because the technology the depart-ment was applying was disconnected from the rest of the company. And the true irony is that the employees of this department never noticed that their actions had no effect on reality.

The moral is obvious: An IS organization that loses touch with its clients will be playing with a technology that has become disconnected from the rest of the corporation. When that happens, it won't be long before the IS personnel also become disconnected from the corporation.

Perception is a curious thing. Even if our clients' perception of IS is inaccurate, their perception is our reality. We're stuck with it. And it affects our ability to work effectively within the organization. If you doubt that statement, try to remember the last time you voluntarily assigned an important project to someone who gave you bad vibes.

We need our clients because they are the only effective judge of our IS organization's value. What creates value in the eyes of the client or potential client? Not technology itself. The client isn't buying hardware or software. He or she is buying the solution to a problem. As long as they get their solution, they don't care if you do it with a Ouija board and pixie dust.

The client is interested only in the technology's features ("What does the product do for me?") and benefits ("What do I get out of it?"). And for the benefit to be real, it must be perceived as such by the client. In fact, a perceived benefit may be more compelling to the client than a real one. As Charles Revson of the Revlon empire once noted, "In the factory we make cosmetics. In the store we sell hope."

Chapter 14

Marketing Techniques: Spreading the Word

Even the best plan degenerates into work.

—Anonymous

If a marketing plan is going to be anything more than a theoretical exercise, at some point the IS organization must move from planning to execution. You have pinpointed your target audiences. You understand their needs. You know the message you want to get across to these audiences. Now comes the moment of truth, the recognition that you can't stand on the high board forever. It's time to plunge into the hands-on world of marketing communications.

Marketing communications is the bridge between the marketing plan and the audience. It's the creation of information vehicles to get your message to that audience. The process involves both form and content—the medium and the message.

The Message

By now you should have your message nailed down. The message involves not only what you plan to tell your target audience but also the marketing objective, the response or desired action you would like to get from your audience. It's not enough to tell your

117

potential clients how wonderful IS is, all the swell services you provide, and how your clients are all now experiencing the good life because of their dealings with IS. The audience reaction is likely to be "So. . . ?"

That's because telling your audience all the wonderful things that IS can do for them is like saying "Be of good cheer" to someone who comes to you with a problem. It's a nice sentiment, laden with warm fuzzies, but it doesn't give much in the way of a practical solution.

To get the potential client to respond, you must communicate your marketing objective: What do you want the target audience to do, not do, let you do? Most marketing programs that fail do so because they are unclear on this question.

The Medium

Once you know your message, there are a million ways of communicating it—from full-page ads in *Fortune* to Freudian slips of paper in fortune cookies. Furthermore, all marketing communications vehicles, if done right, can work. Which ones will work for you? There are two answers:

1. *As many as possible.* Chapter 2 pointed out that people are reluctant to change. They try desperately to maintain the status quo until enough anomalies pile up to overwhelm it. Only then will they accept your technology . . . because it appears to solve the problem created by the anomalies. Thus, the more communications vehicles you use, the easier it is to surround your audience with a new reality—your message—until that message sinks in.

2. *The ones that are appropriate to your audience, message, budget, image, and corporate norms.*

In choosing your media, a disregard for any of these factors is tantamount to hitting the self-destruct button for your marketing program. Let's consider some examples of each:

- *Your audience.* If your target is your company's publications department, its staff is likely to be visually sophisticated. Elaborate and even flashy computer graphics would appeal to their creative instincts. That same look would probably raise eyebrows in the accounting department (although we've known some wild and crazy accountants). When a stereotype conflicts with your actual knowledge of the target audience, deep-six the stereotype and go with reality.

- *Your message.* A trader at the Chicago Board Options Exchange once did a needlepoint of the logo of every company on which the exchange traded options. The needlepoint was huge and very well done. Someone suggested using it as the cover of the annual report. Nope. Because that was the year the Exchange moved into its new building, loaded with state-of-the-art computer trading technology, the theme of the annual report was to stress the exchange as the high-tech financial marketplace. Needlepoint would have conveyed exactly the opposite message, old-fashioned hand craftsmanship.

- *Your budget.* Your company and/or industry is going through a cyclical economic downturn. Your message is that IS technology can help the various departments cut costs without cutting back on service. The last thing in the world you would want to do is use a very expensive vehicle (say, an elaborate and lavish four-color brochure) to convey your belt-tightening-through-technology message.

- *Your image.* If IS has a negative image in your corporation, be careful not to do anything that reinforces that image. If IS is perceived as never delivering anything on time and you commit to a series of informational presentations to middle management, don't allow anything short of a direct hit by a nuclear warhead to cause any of the presentation dates to be rescheduled.

- *Corporate norms.* What's acceptable to your corporation? Tie-dyed, heavy metal-style T-shirts emblazoned with "IS: We fondle floppies" might be just the thing for IS people to hand out . . . if they were working for a rock record label. On the other hand, an insurance company might not be amused. On a somewhat less extreme level, there are lethal ramifications to using your corporate logo, and many corporations insist upon approving all printed materials bearing their name. Go through channels if appropriate.

Potential Pitfalls

The objective of marketing communications is for IPPs to market the IS organization, staff, products, and services—the business benefits that IS can provide—not to market themselves. The development of a "we" attitude, a team approach that spreads with each encounter, is essential to success. This is one activity in which individuals within IS cannot afford to march to a different drummer. Self-aggrandizement by any one IS staff member could prove fatal to the entire marketing plan, which will then be viewed not as an attempt to help clients or the corporation but to boost one egomaniac's career.

A second glaring mistake often made in marketing communications—and it's one that even marketing professionals are occasionally guilty of—is to focus on the IS organization instead of your audience.

In the same year that the American colonies were declaring their independence from England, the Scottish economist Adam Smith published *The Wealth of Nations*. In it, he reminded us that "It is not from the benevolence of the butcher, the brewer or the baker that we expect our dinner, but from their regard for their own self-interest. We address ourselves not to their humanity, but to their self-love, and never talk to them of our own necessities, but of their advantage."

Your IS organization may be the greatest thing to have happened to computers since the transistor. Boring. No one cares. Your clients are interested only in what you can do for them.

The third marketing communications trap is the marketing equivalent of deciding on technology before you analyze the problem. In marketing it takes the form of picking a communications vehicle before you think through the audience and the message. Someone says, "Hey! We've got a great new service here. Let's tell the world about it! Let's do a brochure!" Maybe. Maybe not. What if it's the kind of thing that has to be demonstrated or explained in person? Consider how the people in your audience like to receive information. Do they like position papers? Give them a position paper. Do they like slide presentations? Drag out the projector. Do they like stained glass windows? Forget it. You've got a budget, remember?

All marketing communications vehicles can work—and work well. But that doesn't mean they are all equal. In a given situation, what makes one work while another crashes is the match-up between the medium, on the one hand, and the message, budget, and audience, on the other.

To help IS organizations in the selection process, for each of the marketing communications vehicles I discuss, I spell out its intended audience, advantages and disadvantages, appropriate situations for using it, and tips on increasing its effectiveness.

When you do it right, selecting the right communications vehicle offers the IS free credibility, visibility, and publicity. Let's take a look at some of the techniques that have been used in many IS organizations with great success. Not all of these applications will be right for your organization. Feel free to discard those. Nor is this a complete list. You may come up with others on your own, and if so, please write and let me know. We have divided marketing techniques into two categories: print and nonprint. Chapters 15 and 16 will discuss each of these in detail and will include specific examples.

Chapter 15

The Printed Word

A powerful agent is the right word. Whenever we come upon one of those intensely right words in a book or newspaper the resulting effect is physical as well as spiritual, and electrically prompt.

—*Mark Twain*

There's something about seeing it on paper that somehow makes it more real. Let's look at official written communications that could and most likely will help market your IS organization.

A Mission Statement

A mission statement, which describes the role and goals of an organization, can be your most important marketing tool. It's also one of the most overlooked. If it exists at all, it is likely to be not well-publicized, not accurate, or not revised often enough to reflect changes in the organization. Also, there is frequently a great deal of grass-roots resistance to the whole idea of a mission statement. Behind this opposition is the notion that a mission statement is some kind of highfalutin MBA nonsense that has nothing to do with how the real world works. When verbalized, this attitude is usually expressed as some form of "Cut the bull. Just let me do my job."

The problem with that sentiment is that, without a mission statement, you might not know what your job really is. Thus, the

IS organization should have its own mission statement, one that derives from the corporation's overall mission statement. The more that the mission statement helps IS focus concretely on its role within the organization, the more effective IS can be. Thus a good mission statement should tell you at all times where IS is headed. A great mission statement should tell you what to do when you get to work on Monday morning.

When used to its best advantage, a mission statement creates an awareness of the IS organization's key position in a corporation while preventing project overload by setting goals, boundaries, standards, and realistic expectations. It also keeps the IS organization's team heading in one direction by clearly defining what services it will offer and which ones it will not.

This clearly is important to the IS staff, but the mission statement can also be an effective marketing tool. The IS mission should be posted throughout the corporation so that all employees and officers know about the IS organization's contribution. It should be reexamined every six months and updated if necessary. Here's what you do:

- Think it through. Really think it through.
- Post it.
- Commit to it.
- Establish an IS charter (which sets forth how IS will accomplish its mission).
- Set goals, boundaries, standards, expectations.
- Update this regularly.

What are its advantages?

- It's "official."
- It builds a cohesive team (especially if "they" helped develop the statement).
- It provides focus.
- It pinpoints meaningful objectives.
- It clarifies the goals and objectives of IS.
- It's constantly visible.
- It can be updated.

And its possible disadvantages?

- The IS organization must live up to the expectations that the mission statement creates.
- IS will be judged against the mission statement.
- A good mission statement is tough to generate.
- There is always the danger of your mission statement becoming outdated, even obsolete.
- It needs constant reinforcement, both with IS people and throughout the rest of the organization.
- It can be too lofty to be useful. ("We will be the best IS organization in the known universe.")
- If not worded precisely, it can be subject to misinterpretation.

You can increase its effectiveness by:

- Reviewing the mission statement yearly.
- Keeping it current.
- Recognizing that it is not written in marble.
- Tying it in with the corporate mission statement.

Brochures

When you reach the point where you're frequently repeating the same information but to different people, perhaps the information should be in a printed format. In large organizations, a pocket-sized brochure can serve both as a handy reference guide for those already familiar with IS services and as a quick introduction to those unfamiliar with IS. You can provide three things in the brochure (or, depending on the organization and how much you have to say, perhaps in three separate brochures):

1. *An expanded IS organizational chart,* showing the various functional units, what each does, how they relate to each other, and how they relate to the company.

2. *A client's guide to IS–land.* Some potential clients out there

might benefit from a LAN (local area network), for example, but don't know what it is. A simple explanation of your principal products and services might be in order.

3. *The questions most frequently asked by IS clients.* You'll probably get a lot more mileage out of this one if you print the answers too.

A brochure need not be elaborate, but it does have to be clear and comprehensible. Like the mission statement, the brochure should be reviewed frequently and revised as needed. An out-of-date brochure makes IS look as bad as out-of-date technology would.

The potential audience for brochures includes both internal and external clients and all new employees. They are most appropriate in large, diverse organizations and in organizations where there are many levels of technical sophistication.

What are the advantages of a brochure?

- It's good public relations, providing IS with visibility.
- It's easy reading (or should be).

And its possible disadvantages?

- There's no feedback.
- It has a limited life before technology and organizational change render it obsolete.
- It might require many versions.
- Depending on the degree of elaborateness, it could get expensive.

You can further increase the effectiveness of a brochure by:

- Using photographs (if appropriate).
- Planting subtle, subliminal messages in it.
- Making it enticing and easy to read.
- Using color.
- Customizing it for a specific targeted audience.
- Posting it.

An IS Newsletter

A newsletter to clients is a good place in which to publicize the effective uses of information technologies that are available to clients. The newsletter is not a place for internal IS technology updates, nor a place for IPPs to spotlight themselves. Instead, articles must focus on the client and on business payoffs from working with IS. Clients should be encouraged to contribute articles that tell their own stories.

An IS newsletter should have two goals:

1. To provide clients and potential clients with information of value to them. This will improve the perception of IS.
2. To remind business clients of IS's accessibility and capabilities. This will increase IS visibility.

The newsletter doesn't have to be flashy and expensive, but it should reflect the professionalism and responsiveness of the IS organization it represents. Match the format and appearance to your audience. If you arrive at an effective format, leave it in place to establish some continuity, but nothing is carved in stone. Don't be afraid to change the format every couple of years if you sense that the newsletter is losing reader interest. But first make sure that the problem is format boredom, not content boredom.

Once started, a newsletter should be kept up. Clients will come to count on it and should not be let down. For the same reason, once you decide on a publishing schedule, stick to it. It's now the publishing equivalent of ROM (read only memory). Whatever publication frequency you choose—I suggest quarterly or bimonthly as best—if an issue is supposed to be out on June 1, make it happen. Better yet, get it to your clients a couple of days ahead of schedule.

The newsletter represents a commitment to business clients. Your IS reputation is riding on it. You don't want to give potential clients the opportunity to reject you by saying, "How can I trust them with a major project? They can't even get a little newsletter out on time."

Finally, if for any reason an IS newsletter is unfeasible, try for an occasional "Info Systems Corner" column in your company's management newsletter or customer or employee publications. For a newsletter, the entire corporation is your audience, and it will be especially welcome whenever a reorganization or major changes are going on.

What are a newsletter's advantages?

- It's informative.
- It's visible.
- It achieves employee recognition.
- It's current.
- It reaches a large audience.
- It's cost-effective.

And its possible disadvantages?

- A newsletter is labor-intensive.
- It gets little feedback.
- It has no depth.
- It can carry only enough information to whet the reader's appetite.
- It's difficult to judge its effectiveness.

You could further increase the effectiveness of a newsletter by:

- Targeting your audience.
- Offering it on-line.
- Providing phone numbers of key IS contacts.
- Providing references.
- Including an IS management summary.
- Knowing your clients' needs.

Management Reports

One of the best forms of marketing IS is a carefully planned and produced annual or semiannual management report. This is a combination annual report and state-of-the-union message that highlights key accomplishments since the previous report and discusses plans for the next reporting period. The key to an effective report is to base it on evaluation of hard business results. To accomplish this, the IPP must work with every client to establish evaluation criteria for the success of significant projects.

This must be done before each project begins. Establishing measurable results criteria in advance is important for two reasons:

1. Deciding on how you will evaluate results while the project is in progress or, even worse, after it's finished is naive and ineffective. At their worst, such after-the-fact measurement systems turn out to be ineffective. Wait to see what happens and then announce that this was the result you wanted. It's like throwing the dart and then drawing a bull's-eye around it.

2. Having preproject measurement criteria also serves to protect IS from its clients. Down the road no one can change the ground rules for scoring on you. Revisit the project with the client three to six months after project completion to perform the evaluation. An evaluation made by the client rather than by IS alone is more convincing.

Ideally, the part of the management report that addresses the future should be tied to the operating plans of the organization's functional areas. The IPP can work with managers of these areas to define priorities among their business goals and to determine the areas in which IPPs can work as partners in meeting those goals. Of course, this must be a realistic assessment, because this report section should be revisited in the next management report to evaluate success against the plan.

The form this report takes depends on the organization's culture. In a company that is very presentation-oriented, the IPP should develop a concise management presentation that can be delivered in person. For greatest impact, the presentation should also be given to senior management. In organizations with a less formal and more participative culture, the management report may be an opportunity to build a working relationship with senior management. In this vein, the IPP can prepare an informal set of flip charts or a working document to be used as the basis for a brainstorming session with key managers to get their input on future directions. An assessment of past directions and accomplishments serves as an effective introduction to or refresher on what the IPP does and can stimulate creative ideas on how to build partnerships on key initiatives.

If the corporation is large and the culture formal, it may be most effective to make the management report into a professionally produced document that can be distributed to the management hierarchy. Or this approach can be combined with the others. Whatever format you use, the goal is to increase upper-level management's awareness of IS activities and of their value to the organization.

What are the advantages of a management report?

- It provides a summary of what IS has accomplished.
- It also provides an overview of where IS is headed.
- It's an effective vehicle for sharing information with a large client base.
- It's an opportunity to reflect on trends.
- It's portable.
- It has the potential for multimedia applicability.
- It offers recipients a convenient reference.

And its possible disadvantages?

- The report will be meaningless unless you provide enough information and detail.
- Dated material can nullify the usefulness of a report.
- Significant problems are often hidden by such reports.
- There may be a temptation to go for "glitz"—all smoke and mirrors, with no substance.
- There's rarely any feedback.
- Preparing the report is a time-consuming process.

You could further increase the effectiveness of a management report by:

- Utilizing mixed media (speeches, slides, print handouts).
- Offering the full report on a take-home disk.
- Soliciting client feedback.

- Relating the report to business benefits.
- Making it eye-catching.

5/15 Reports

These are brief monthly "insider reports" to upper-level management that can serve as interim updates of the last major management report. They should cover the same topics but in a highly condensed fashion. Honesty is critical. They are called 5/15 reports because they should take only five minutes to read and fifteen minutes to write.

The 5/15 report is also a great way to keep the IS team members in tune with each other. This is critical because an IS marketing plan will not fly if the organization isn't sending a consistent message to clients.

What are the advantages of a 5/15 report?

- It provides a summary of what IS has accomplished.
- It also provides an overview of where IS is headed.
- It's an effective vehicle for sharing information with a large client base.
- It's an opportunity to reflect trends.
- It's portable.
- The collected reports serve as the foundation for your next annual management report.

And its possible disadvantages?

- Rehashing old news may hurt IS credibility.
- So will a lack of candor.

You could further increase its effectiveness by:

- Soliciting market user feedback.
- Relating the report to business benefits.
- Making it eye-catching.

External Publications

Newspapers, the business press, technical publications, and the trade press can offer free publicity to those with an interesting story to tell. Effective use of this free exposure can benefit all involved—clients, the IPPs who assisted them, the corporation, and the publication. When IPPs hear of some of the great things that clients are doing with information technologies, they should get the details and try to get them published. Enlist the aid of your corporation's public relations people. They are always on the lookout for a good story to bring to the media and they know the ropes of dealing with editors and reporters.

Please note that there are no guarantees that a publication will pick up the story. Editors cannot be bribed or bullied into printing something that doesn't grab them. But most people like a success story.

If you do succeed in getting something published, you not only get the initial benefit of seeing it in print, but there's an even bigger payoff. You can reprint the article as an inexpensive—and highly effective—marketing handout.

The advantage to external publication (and reprints) is the third-party credibility it offers. If you say that IS technology is great, it has less effect because it sounds self-serving. Clients expect you to say that. But if a newspaper or trade magazine says the same thing, it now has more impact. The subconscious impact on clients, both potential and actual, is "They must be good or the magazine wouldn't have printed it." Your company's external customers will also take notice.

In additional to external publications, try for your company publications. The impact's not the same, but it's still worthwhile.

What are the advantages of external publication?

- Publication by a noncompany source adds third-party credibility.
- The original article can be turned into inexpensive reprints, a highly effective marketing tool for IS.
- The initial publication of the article and the reprints generate client support.

And the possible disadvantages?

- You have no control over what use, if any, the publication will make of the information you provide.
- You have to be in the right publication, one that your target audience reads, for maximum effect. If the only magazine your clients read is *Soybean Quarterly*, that's the one you should shoot for.
- If, for some reason, the editors of a publication choose not to use your "great story," this can be very disappointing because you have put a lot of work and time into it.

You could further increase the effectiveness of external publication by:

- *Suiting the story to the publication.* Getting into *The Wall Street Journal* might be highly prestigious, but that newspaper probably won't be interested in a new internal software program for your accounting department. However, trade magazines that cover the computer and accounting industries might be.
- *Checking out the publication before you make contact.* You need to know what kinds of stories it runs. Ninety percent of the unsolicited material received by editors is rejected because it's inappropriate for the publication. It might be a good story but not for that particular publication. You never should have sent it there in the first place.
- *Sending the publication a query first.* This is simply a phone call or letter outlining the story you are proposing and telling why you think it's significant, or at least interesting. This allows the editors to make a spot evaluation without wasting their time or yours.
- *Getting help with the writing.* Your PR people will be glad to help. If they aren't available, hire a free-lance writer. Doing this is surprisingly inexpensive and will greatly improve the story.
- *Include good photos.* These always help.
- *Suiting the technical sophistication of the article to the publication's readership.* Readers of a computer trade magazine might

want all the nuts and bolts specs of how your new application works. And they will understand the technical terminology. Readers of an accounting trade magazine won't know or care. They would be interested only in what it might do for them.

Chapter 16

Nonprint Communication Vehicles

It is said that the world is run by those willing to sit until the end of meetings.

—Hugh Park

Walk-In Center

In an era of end-user technology, an ongoing walk-in center, where clients on all levels can see the available and/or supported information technologies and ask questions about them, is an effective way to promote IS capabilities, and to build strong community awareness.

A walk-in center does not require a spacious first-floor room with marble walls and plush carpeting. However, it should be easily accessible to potential business clients. What makes a walk-in center effective is a professional approach by the IS staff. The client should feel comfortable in a walk-in center. A general presentation should be given to each first-time visitor. His or her specific needs should be addressed only if the client is ready to discuss specifics. This is your opportunity to make a great first impression. Don't blow it.

As a resource center for clients, the walk-in center can offer a publications library, equipment loans, demonstrations, evaluations, and testing. The center has the added advantage of allowing IS to leverage expensive equipment. However, the staff should concentrate on being helpful and remembering that this is a client center, not a product center. In many corporations, the walk-in center has created a big market for basic PC training among the corporation's non-IS staff. But it should go much beyond the PC training. For example, discuss such items as telecommunication architecture, database administration, and futuristic tools and applications.

What are the advantages of a walk-in center?

- It's a ready resource for your company.
- It's convenient; no appointments are necessary.
- It provides a showroom for the efficient use of special equipment and for the skills of your people.
- It helps both IS and the company to identify opportunities and needs.
- It improves relationships with clients.
- It provides clients with hands-on access to new technology.
- An ad hoc approach gives IS the flexibility to deal with specific needs and problems.
- The personal one-on-one service reduces a visitor's potential embarrassment. (It's a lot easier for people to admit they don't understand a word of what you're saying if there's not a crowd around.)

And its possible disadvantages?

- It's expensive, requiring space, staff, and equipment.
- It requires management attention to keep the center up to date.
- If your company has multiple locations, the walk-in center can't service the remote operations.
- If the IS center is too successful, you could have clients queuing up for your services. And no one enjoys waiting in line.
- The center staff could start to view itself as an IS elite.

- The walk-in center could turn into a development center, where clients come regularly to develop their personal applications.
- Walk-in centers often tend to be desktop-focused.

You could further increase its effectiveness by:

- Helping clients to solve their own problems.
- Broadening available service—to include R&D, for instance.
- Rotating the center's staff.
- Providing the center's staff with training in people skills.
- Being realistic in what you can and cannot offer.
- Advertising the center's existence (on bulletin boards, in your newsletter, in the company publication).
- Offering amenities such as comfortable chairs, coffee, food.

Scheduled (and Unscheduled) Presentations

Such presentations can take a number of different formats. Let's take a look at a few varieties of this marketing vehicle.

Presentations to Potential Clients

A presentation to a business organization within the corporation is one of the best approaches to spreading the IS message while simultaneously establishing personal contact with potential clients. With a minimal time investment, IPPs can put together ready-to-go presentations on such topics as:

- Who are we?
- What is our role or mission?
- What services do we provide?
- Who's on staff, and what are their qualifications?
- Where do we fit on the organization chart?
- What do we require from our clients?
- How have we helped our clients to solve business problems?
- What are the best ways of utilizing IS?

Each member of the staff should play a role in the presentation and be able to fill in whenever necessary. Keep the language nontechnical. If you can't avoid introducing technical terms, then you must explain them. The emphasis should be on services and solutions, not specific products, although a product overview may be helpful near the end.

The obvious place to start is by determining which people on the IS staff are skilled speakers—or could be with a little practice. Don't eliminate a candidate because of sweaty palms. After all, we're talking about a collection of introverts here. But IPPs are not alone. The general public ranks speaking in public as their number one fear—more so than death, which ranks a distant fourth. In short, most people would rather die than give a speech. And even one of the world's greatest actors, the late Sir Laurence Olivier, suffered so from stage fright throughout his career that he was known to vomit before going on stage.

So don't think that a little nervousness disqualifies you or anyone else in IS. Instead, invest in a little presentation training, if necessary, and involve the IS staff. Even if they can't all be speakers, they can always serve as an audience for practice runs.

When your speakers are ready, turn them loose with a mission: to educate people about IS and its services. Your audiences will be clients and potential clients from your corporation (probably on the executive or managerial level), but don't overlook the possibility of external audiences (that is, local IS groups, associations, chambers of commerce). In fact, if an IS person makes a speech to an outside group, maximize the exposure by publicizing it within the company.

Whether external or internal, the presentations themselves should emphasize services and solutions, not products. Speakers should remember that they are speaking to businessmen and women and not to fellow IPPs. Use business rather than technical language or you may find yourself addressing an audience that fervently wishes your talk came with subtitles.

What are the advantages of a client presentation?

- A speech is a direct, effective form of communication.
- It provides personal, face-to-face contact.
- It can whet the potential client's appetite for IS services.

- Telling the IS story to an entire group saves time.
- Because the speech is prepared in advance and in writing, the message is consistent no matter how many times it is presented.
- By watching the audience reaction and taking questions, you get instant feedback.
- Speeches provide IS with visibility.
- You know you are reaching your target audience.
- The presentation gives potential clients the opportunity to talk to IS.

And its possible disadvantages?

- A speech takes a lot of preparation and time.
- You may select the wrong person as a speaker to represent IS.
- Scheduling speeches is always difficult because of the problem of finding a time when everyone is free.
- The audience may be hostile. That can be disconcerting to the speaker.
- You can't divide and conquer. The speech format doesn't allow you the opportunity of winning the battle by making individual converts on a one-on-one basis.
- The message may be too generic to be helpful to the audience.
- No matter how carefully you schedule, there will always be some people who can't make it. Thus, the message won't always reach everyone you would like to get it to.

You could increase the effectiveness of your client presentation by:

- Following up the presentation by later making individual contact with those in the audience.
- Targeting the presentation to the needs of the group you are speaking to.
- Keeping your speech as short as possible. (It's bad enough when those in the audience start looking at their watches.

When they start shaking their watches to see if they're still working, it's definitely time for the speaker to sit down.)
- Letting a client who is a convert to IS make the presentation.
- Utilizing good audiovisuals.
- Encouraging audience participation.

Brown Bag Seminars

Another option for an IS presentation is what is called a brown bag special. This is when IPPs schedule a presentation in a conference room or client site to be given during the lunch period. Clients and others can relax and listen while eating their brown bag goodies. Sometimes the format is an open house; at other times invitations are sent out to specific guests. The setting is informal, and no demands are made on attendees. The presentation can introduce IS to the organization or it can focus on a particular information technology topic. Such seminars are particularly effective when current events have impacted a large segment of the organization.

What are its advantages?

- Open communication is enhanced by a relaxed atmosphere.
- It does not impinge on normal working hours.
- It provides an opportunity to hear other viewpoints.
- There is low overhead.

And its possible disadvantages?

- You may not get the right audience.
- Keeping the meeting in focus can be difficult amidst the rattling of paper bags and the pouring of coffee.
- Your audience may have hidden agendas; for example, people may take advantage of your presence to inform you of negative concerns they may have.
- Those invited may be reluctant to give up their free time.
- You, too, are missing your normal lunch hour.
- Having people from different levels in the same audience can make the presentation awkward because the different levels have different concerns.

You could increase the effectiveness of brown bag specials by:

- Limiting each session to a single topic.
- Holding them more often, repeating specific topics.
- Doing it by invitation only.
- Scheduling the brown bag sessions in advance.
- Having handouts available on the day's topic.
- Varying the sessions in terms of content.
- Budget permitting, providing a simple lunch for participants.

"House Calls"

Another way to market the IS organization is through scheduled meetings with the staffs or management of various departments. Bringing an IS presentation to the client's place of business can be highly effective. IPPs can approach various department managers to find out whether they can introduce the IS organization or end-user computing to each manager's staff. While this may conjure up images of IS as the Avon ladies of technology, many managers will like the idea, and in this way spread the IS message and success story.

Unscheduled House Calls

A variation of the house call, the unscheduled call can be considered one aspect of MBWA (management by walking around). On the way over to the human resources department, you have to pass by engineering anyway. If you know someone there, stop by and spend five minutes: just a quick "Hi!" and a few moments to find out what she's working on and to update her on developments in IS.

This "I-just-happened-to-be-in-the-neighborhood" approach calls for a little sensitivity, of course. If you engineer friend is in the middle of a crisis, feverishly trying to meet a deadline, or happens to have someone else in her office, wave hello and pass on. There will always be another day. This is an excellent "get close to the client" technique that sends a good message to the client.

Both scheduled and unscheduled door-to-door house calls offer the same opportunities, pros and cons. Be very sensitive to your audience and make sure you are welcome. If you sense any hostility, leave. Also keep in mind that although MBWA has received some good press, practicing it takes time away from your duties and must be balanced. You also risk giving the impression that you don't have much else to do.

What are the advantages of house calls?

- They're the most personal form of communication.
- The visits are a good way for you to gain confidence and to increase your people skills.
- One-on-one meetings always reduce the risk of embarrassment.
- House calls are less intimidating to the client.
- You can tailor your approach to each department or even to each individual.
- You personally select your "audience."
- They offer a perfect opportunity for questions and answers.
- They provide wider recognition for IS throughout the organization.

And their possible disadvantages?

- They're time-consuming.
- It's easy for IS to overcommit its resources.
- The first time you meet with a person is like making a cold call.
- The client may not have time to see you and may therefore view your visit as disruptive.

You could further increase the effectiveness of house calls by:

- Networking on a continuing basis.
- Getting to know your clients and their needs.
- Leaving something positive with them.

- Keeping your visit short. If the discussion gets involved and requires more time, make an appointment to come back with more detail.

Presentations to IS Groups

In large organizations, it's important to keep in mind that IS itself is a key audience for your message. Formal presentations to IS colleagues or sister IS organizations are a good way of keeping everyone informed, up to date, and on the same wave length. They also help build team spirit throughout IS. This can become important in major projects that require support from every area of IS. Such presentations are particularly appropriate when organizational changes and technology enhancements need to be discussed.

What are the advantages of presentations to IS groups?

- They serve as a tool for solving internal IS problems.
- They can be more informal, since the audience is already familiar with other areas of IS.
- They help you gain internal support.
- They promote team effort.
- They lessen resistance to change.
- They can help IS to focus on priorities.
- They provide all areas of IS with a broader view of their functions.
- They can help IS identify overlapping activities.
- They can help IS communicate where it is going and help identify problems it might encounter along the way.
- A broader understanding of the total IS picture can help IS staff members identify career paths.

And their possible disadvantages?

- The audience is limited. In a sense, you're talking to yourself.
- Because the focus is narrow, there's a risk of forgetting the business perspective.
- They are time-consuming.

- While you're holding meetings, no one is minding the store and servicing clients.
- If the internal IS problems aren't solved, this puts IS management at risk.

You could further increase their effectiveness by:

- Using high-powered speakers to generate enthusiasm.
- Bringing clients in to present.
- Demanding high-quality presentations.
- Maintaining continuity and frequency.
- Keeping them brief.
- Providing handouts.
- Appointing a contact person to provide more information.

Client Groups

Even if your client loves what IS has done for it, if that client is a lone voice crying in the wilderness, its support will do little to enhance the reputation of IS. But what if you link that client with other IS clients who are using the same IS applications? Two things can come out of such client groups and they are both extremely positive: (1) That lone voice becomes a chorus of support for IS; (2) even more important, as the clients in the group interact, they learn from each other.

By helping to create and support such client groups, IS also creates an atmosphere in which clients assume ownership—and, therefore, support of IS. They are particularly appropriate for introducing new IS products and services, for communicating changes, and for airing or solving problems.

What are the advantages of client groups?

- They bring about networking.
- The groups leverage what others have done.
- They can address issues with a unified voice.
- They are client-oriented.
- They provide a feedback mechanism.

- They serve as a vehicle for the exchange of information.
- They identify needs and solve problems.

And their possible disadvantages?

- Client group meetings can turn into gripe sessions.
- They may not bring forth a response to issues.
- They offer limited participation.
- It's hard to find dynamic IS leaders to conduct them.
- They are difficult to organize and get going.

You could further increase their effectiveness by:

- Producing client group newsletters.
- Demonstrating tangible results.
- Addressing high-interest topics.
- Using outside speakers.
- Coming in with specific agendas.
- Getting vendor input.
- Offering food and beverages.

User Coordinators

When you plan or design new technological solutions for clients, or introduce a technological system to them for the first time, they are often left with the feeling that IS should also have given them a large red button emblazoned with the word "PANIC!" Murphy's Law dictates that things that can go wrong will go wrong. The attitude of the client toward your technology will hinge directly on the effectiveness of IS procedures in responding to such problems. This is particularly true when the client has a relatively low level of technical sophistication.

One of the best ways to deal with this scenario is to appoint user coordinators. These are IS staff people who have responsibility for assisting specific clients. The user coordinator becomes familiar with the people using the technology, their business needs, and the problems they face with the technology.

When a problem does arise, the client has a specific person to turn to for help. This can considerably raise the client's comfort level by giving technology a human face.

Since IS staff people are only human and sometimes insist on taking sick days and vacation days, it's a good idea to name and train a backup user coordinator. If you don't, I guarantee that Murphy's Law will automatically kick in, decreeing that the client's system will crash only on those days when the user coordinator is not available.

It's also a good idea to have the client group appoint a primary contact with the user coordinator—preferably the person in the client group who is most familiar or most comfortable with the technology. Again, there should be a backup person if the client contact is gone.

This procedure eliminates situations in which the entire panicked client department—not unlike the lynch mob in *The Ox-Bow Incident*—storms IS.

User coordinators are particularly appropriate for liaison with key client organizations and departments with communication problems, and whenever a new system is installed.

What are the advantages of having user coordinators?

- They help bridge the communications gap.
- The system provides cross-training. The client gets needed technological expertise, and the user coordinator becomes familiar with the client's business area.
- The user coordinator is dedicated to the client.
- The setup offers a single point of contact.
- The user coordinator serves as a buffer in disputes over ownership rights.
- IS is provided with a stronger business orientation.
- If the coordinator is placed on the client's payroll, IS's overhead is reduced.

And the possible disadvantages?

- The user coordinator may become a middle man, preventing broader contact between IS and the client.
- The system could separate IS and the true client.

- Too many links can cause distortion of the message.
- The coordinator may acquire too many responsibilities.
- There's danger that this could become a political assignment.
- The system can degenerate into being a "help desk" rather than a strategic focus.
- The coordinator may "go native," that is, come to identify more with the client than with IS, and thereafter put its interests above those of his original department.

Technology/Productivity Fair

This is a more formal extension of the walk-in center, and its purpose is likewise educational. Instead of waiting for potential clients to come to you, put on a show of what IS and technology can do for their productivity. Those invited can see demonstrations of technology and even try using it themselves. Your potential audience is a big one—including middle managers and executives, potential clients, new employees, the whole community in fact.

This hands-on approach raises comfort levels and stimulates ideas for applications. Any time you provide a value-added tip or service, your image goes up a notch.

But don't kid yourself. A productivity fair means setting aside space, time, money, and people to plan and staff it. In short, it's a lot of hard work. But it's also a dramatic way to showcase your IS organization and technology. One of my clients invested more than 2,000 hours preparing for a five-day "Internal Conference" that involved six fifty-minute presentations every day. The bottom line was that the benefits far outweighed the costs.

What are the advantages of a productivity fair?

- It offers indiscriminate marketing.
- It generates awareness of different products and services and gives people a hands-on opportunity to see how they work.
- It showcases successes and capabilities.
- Presenters learn more about their own products and services and the ever-changing world of IS.

- It facilitates the exchange of ideas both within IS and with clients.
- IS staff people who participate have an opportunity to identify with the department as a whole and to function as team members who are making an impact and contributing to the company.
- Presenters with expertise in a particular area are given a chance to shine and to win recognition.
- It offers variety in one place and within a short time span.
- It's a way to promote IS while communicating its direction. This will improve the image of IS.
- It brings IS and clients together.

And its possible disadvantages?

- It requires a substantial investment of resources (space, staff, money).
- It can become focused on presentation rather than on the technology itself.
- It can create false expectations.
- There's always the chance of power or hardware failures making IS look bad.
- There are inherent geographic problems if your company has more than one location. Road shows are impractical.

You could further increase its effectiveness by:

- Not letting demos turn into extended training sessions.
- Introducing new and innovative technology.
- Targeting organizational issues.
- Having clients participate or demonstrate.
- Bringing in qualified vendors.
- Having keynote speakers.
- Offering refreshments and a door prize.
- Conducting a feedback survey.

Marketing a Technological Solution

This time the gods of microchips are kind: The new project works even better than anticipated and IS has on its hands a certifiable success story relevant to your organization and its clients. What do you do? Promote it like crazy, of course. How? All of the above, through every communications technique you can think of. But stick to the facts and the business results. IS will gain credibility if you don't overstate your successes or sweep the failures under the rug.

Now that we have looked at some potential marketing practices, let's look at refining the approach even further. You want more of a return on your investment, don't you?

Chapter 17

What the Pros Know

Good communication is characterized by providing employees with information they want and getting information to them quickly and through channels they prefer.

— Louis I. Gelfand

Every profession has its insider knowledge or tricks of the trade that make life easier for its practitioners. You too can use what marketing communications pros know to improve the quality of your IS marketing materials.

Graphics

When you are going to make a presentation, put a lot of thought into the graphics you use. Good graphics—whether used on slides, overhead transparencies, flip charts, or handouts—don't have to be expensive, but they are worth every cent you do spend. Why? There are two reasons:

1. Quality packaging of your ideas demonstrates that they are important to you.
2. Some graphic specialists believe that meetings are 28 percent shorter when information is presented in graphic form. The clarity of graphics results in faster decision making. So unless you feel that you're just not spending enough of your life at meetings. . . .

The Virtue of Simplicity

Don't confuse simplicity with simplemindedness. Downplay the technical jargon and use short words instead of big words. Nobody makes points by writing *circumstantiation* when *fact* is more than adequate to carry the meaning. This is particularly true respecting communications intended for rank-and-file employees. As much as one-fifth of the adult American population is functionally illiterate. Since our public school system seems to be going down the tubes, we can expect that percentage to increase . . . even as we are faced with a need for employees to fill ever more technologically demanding positions. Here are some recent horror stories:

- One advertiser found that 43 percent of tested consumers didn't understand the word *obsolete*.
- A brewery learned that many of its beer buyers thought that *lagered* meant "tired."
- Procter & Gamble dropped the word *concentrated* from its ads because so many readers thought it meant "blessed by the Pope."
- A survey of high school students indicated that the majority of them thought that "Chernobyl" was Cher's full name.

Sound ridiculous? It is. Unfortunately, these stories are true. The point of all IS communications is to educate and motivate. The most successful communications are those that use simple, easy-to-understand language.

"Ubi Est Meum?"

Roughly translated from the Latin, this means "What's in it for me?" This is the question that every communication to clients or potential clients must answer after you've answered their first question, "What do you want me to do?"

Emotion

This is a touchy issue. Rationality doesn't motivate human behavior. Emotion does. You doubt that? OK, let's have a debate, with the audience to pick the winner. You choose the topic. Doesn't matter to me. Furthermore, I'll concede to you the use of all facts, statistics, logic, and rationality. I, in turn, will use a graphic: a Norman Rockwell picture of a little boy with freckles, a baseball glove, a bandage on his knee, and a puppy dog. Result: I'll give you and your statistics a good run for your money.

So you have a great deal to gain from using emotion effectively. There's just one problem: Organizations don't like using emotion. They are uncomfortable with the idea. Also, people know when you're using emotion and feel manipulated.

The obvious solution is to combine emotion with reason. Give people a rational reason (permission) for doing what you made them want to do emotionally. Just like you bought that little red convertible sports car because it gets 28 miles to the gallon. Oh, sure.

Using Words With Impact

Words are like software. Some work better than others. They have more impact, so they get results. Other words are a turnoff. They have a negative impact on your chances of getting a positive result from the communication. For example, people are more receptive to "We are open till 5 P.M." than to "We close at 5 P.M." For your consideration, here are some lists with samples of words and what we feel about them:

PERSUASIVE WORDS

now	*amazing*
announcing	*bargain*
introducing	*hurry*
improvement	*suddenly*
challenge	*startling*
wanted	*miracle*

easy   magic
compare   offer
revolutionary   free
remarkable   quick
sensational

WORDS WE LIKE

success   pleasure
positive self-image   freedom
social acceptance   security
comfort   health
recognition   love

WORDS WE DISLIKE

conflict   loneliness
pain   sickness
trouble

WORDS WE PREFER

you   money
your   people
how   now
new   want
who   why

Try these substitutions for a more positive effect:

INSTEAD OF   TRY:

problem   opportunity
conflict   challenge
change   enhancement
I   we

The One-on-One Approach

One of the deep, dark secrets of public relations is that there are
no publics. Even when using the mass media, you're still talking

to one person at a time. Bigger audiences just mean that you have to generalize more to make your message relevant. What interests the accounting people may bore production or customer service. And vice versa. The more people you try to talk to at the same time, the less you have to say to any of them . . . until you have nothing to say to everyone. The more you can target specific groups, the more effective you will be. And the most effective communication is you and the client chatting over a cup of coffee.

Keeping Your Marketing Plan on Track

There are seven critical stages in any effective marketing communications program:

1. *Planning.* Of content, format, budget, responsibilities. This is where things start to fall between the cracks.

2. *Selling your plans and ideas.* These should be presold to your management as part of the overall marketing plan. They should also be sold to your staff and the people in any other department on whom you may have to call for support (publications, PR, marketing, and so forth).

3. *Assigning tasks.* Who does what? Be specific. The Mensa Clubs of two cities once decided to have their memberships meet at the halfway point for a chili cookout at which they could admire each other's superior intellects. They forgot the chili.

4. *Supervising execution.* This is especially critical in that it may get the IS organization involved in areas that it's not familiar with (such as speech making, graphics, printing). This is the IS manager's role and it's no time for management by exception. It's hands-on all the way.

5. *Doing the tasks.* You may do some of this yourself. You may delegate some of it to your staff. But get it done, or remain nose-deep in theoretical marketing.

6. *Managing the budget.* Marketing, like every other corporate activity, is a business function. You should be in a position to tell your management exactly what your marketing program cost and what the payback was (or is projected to be).

7. *Evaluation.* The evaluation phase begins before the marketing program itself with the setting of realistic marketing objectives. It begins with asking "How will we know we're successful?" and setting agreed-upon benchmarks. It ends with the final evaluation of the entire program. If your marketing program isn't worth a postmortem, it wasn't worth attempting in the first place.

Chapter 18

Reprogramming IS

However far modern science and technics have fallen short of their inherent possibilities, they have taught mankind at least one lesson: Nothing is impossible.

—*Lewis Mumford*

We mere humans have unprotected memories. It's too easy to forget the important stuff. Fortunately, we have people like Peter Drucker to remind us that "The future will not just happen if one wishes hard enough. It requires decision—now. It imposes risk—now. It requires action—now. It demands allocation of resources, and above all, human resources—now." (From *Money Talks*, New York: Facts on File, 1985)

To IPPs, all this now translates into successful internal marketing of your IS organization. The purpose of this book is to lay out the four keys to marketing success:

1. Creating an awareness of your value
2. Forming partnerships
3. Evolving a promotional strategy
4. Developing long-term client relationships

If that seems like asking a lot, you're right. But unless you're that one person who will make a zillion dollars by figuring out an innovative use for the pinfeed strips on computer paper, consider your only other alternative: the bland mediocrity of working for a second-rate corporation. Count on it.

The successful corporations of the 1990s will be those whose managements have the ability to handle uncertainty. They will be able to combine instinct and intuition with the ability to use computers and telecommunications to assemble and make sense of the information overload that's upon us. We are several generations away from computers programmed for intuition. But the tools IS already has can make our corporations survivors. If—and it's a big if—IPPs have the wisdom to lead their fellow employees to that technology.

The successful companies of the 1990s will share one trait: Each will have an IS organization run by people who have their priorities straight, their direction focused, and their marketing strategy as plugged in as their technology.

Now you know all about marketing. You are a marketing guru. But before you go shouting this from the rooftops, perhaps you should get some practical application under your belt. Simply read (or have your staff read) the following case study. Then, after studying the case, gather around a flip chart or your writing pad and analyze it in terms of the thirteen-step marketing plan detailed in Chapter 12. Fill in what you or your team feels is the correct marketing strategy based on your understanding of the case. Remember, there are no absolutes—anything goes. Be creative, give it a shot, and put into practice what you have learned.

CASE STUDY:
SLEEPY VALLEY VINEYARDS, INC.

Sleepy Valley Vineyards began in 1937 as a small, local winery in the Deep South. Until recently, its production levels were modest when compared to the large California vineyards. The Sleepy Valley label was little known outside a few Southern states.

This began to change rapidly in 1980, after a New York consulting firm convinced Sleepy Valley executives to begin marketing their down-home country image and change their less-than-exciting slogan: "Sleepy Valley Makes Grape Wine." The consultants also encouraged Sleepy Valley executives, mostly descendants of the family that had started the business, to make a substantial investment in advertising its newest product, wine coolers, and to begin selling the product nationally.

With a new image, new slogan, new products, and a new nationwide television advertising campaign, Sleepy Valley's sales soared. In just a decade, revenues grew from $18 million to $240 million. The wine cooler line was expanded. Production and work force totals skyrocketed. Sleepy Valley had emerged as a major player in the wine industry.

Sleepy Valley's boom years were fueled by new products, new ideas, and the public's natural curiosity. The company's biggest concern was not competition but keeping up with demand. Now the boom is over. Sales are leveling off as competitors aggressively attack Sleepy Valley's market share. The company's executives are facing problems they never dreamed of, let alone encountered, when they were a small, local winery. They must now find ways to protect what they've built while battling the competition.

Although Sleepy Valley went public a few dozen years ago, it's still largely controlled by the Hilly family, which founded the company. Members of the second and third generations of the family hold many of the top positions.

The IS Organization

Sleepy Valley's IS organization has played only a minor, background role in the company's recent growth. Over the years, IS has been responsible for automating payroll, implementing office automation, and compiling reports—but for little else. Sleepy Valley is a little company that grew up quickly. The company's executives, who have never attached great value to having up-to-the-minute information, are less than eager to invest in new technologies, especially after watching sales boom without help from all that expensive equipment.

Although IS has had some success with departments like payroll and personnel, most of the people who work in Sleepy Valley's business departments shy away from IS. They feel that dealing with IS is too complicated. They say they have a hard time communicating with IS professionals, many of whom were recruited from the city to work at Sleepy Valley's secluded, rural headquarters. Sleepy Valley's non-IS employees aren't exactly sure what IS can do for them anyway. Some executives, like Sleepy Valley's chief operating officer, have an outright disdain for IS: "IS," he says, "is overhead to the overhead of this company."

The Sleepy Valley IS organization grew during the last decade, along with every other department. Now, however, there's talk that its staff of 175 may be trimmed. The technology IS uses, particularly its mainframe, is generally sufficient, but not necessarily the latest. Its hardware budget has been kept modest.

At the leadership level, IS is aware of its poor image among Sleepy Valley employees. The problem is changing that image, which is especially tricky in that some within the IS organization itself see no reason for changing it. "Why look for more work," they say. "We have enough already."

When IS recently received word that it would be the first department to face cutbacks owing to slowing sales, the IS director decided that changing the organization's image would be his top priority. There's a whole cast of characters he has to deal with.

Jed Hilly, Chief Executive Officer

Jed Hilly, 55, is the youngest of the second generation of the Hilly family. He won the top post after a drawn-out, often bitter battle with his siblings, two of whom left the company as a result. They said Jed Hilly wanted to "citify" the business.

With an MBA degree, Jed Hilly has more formal education than the rest of his family. Like his relatives, however, Jed Hilly still holds traditional values dear. While he will give in to new ideas if there is a strong business case for them, he continues to try to preserve the small family business Sleepy Valley once was—the business he grew up with.

Jed Hilly reports to Sleepy Valley's board of directors.

Bill Hilly, Chief Operations Officer

Bill Hilly, 63, grew up in the barns and vineyards of Sleepy Valley. He feels bitter because his romantic notion of the family business he grew up with has been shattered over the past ten years. A stubborn family elder, Bill Hilly opposes virtually any and all changes in the business. Even though the company's soaring profits have made him a wealthy man, he still lives in the same house and drives the same car he did ten years ago. "Some things mean more than money," he grumbles. "And some things shouldn't change."

Bill Hilly attempts to maintain tight control over the departments that report to him, but his stubbornness has eroded some of the loyalty he once commanded. Some department heads have learned that they can accomplish their goals by going directly to Jed Hilly, which infuriates Bill. He feels that there's more than his honor at stake: There's the future of what was once a friendly family business, one that is now on its way to becoming "a conglomerate."

Bill Hilly reports to Chief Executive Officer Jed Hilly.

Sid Slicker, Vice-President of IS

Sid Slicker, 46, is a well-educated, energetic IS veteran who six months ago left a position as IS director of a Boston company to join Sleepy Valley. IS professionals at Sleepy Valley view Slicker's ideas as progressive, even though similar strategies are already being implemented every day at numerous IS organizations, including the one at Slicker's former employer.

Slicker left Boston to escape the frantic city pace and find a more relaxed atmosphere in which to raise his young children. While his wife and children have adapted well to their new environment, Slicker still deals with people in the same way he did in Boston. As a result, many Sleepy Valley employees—even some within the IS organization—see the determined Slicker as pushy, abrasive, and sometimes arrogant.

Slicker has lofty goals for his new IS organization and he's not about to be patient in reaching them. He wants the IS organization to quickly become a major player in the corporation.

Slicker reports to Chief Operations Officer Bill Hilly.

Sam Subdued, IS Client Services Director

Sam Subdued, 57, started working for Sleepy Valley twenty-nine years ago in its tiny data processing shop. He convinced the former VP of IS, a good friend, to promote him to his current position seven years ago. His department has barely changed since. Subdued feels that those with a need for IS services will find him and sees no need to seek out new customers.

A friendly, good-natured man, he gets along well with most Sleepy Valley employees, particularly the veterans. (He hunts with Bill Hilly.) Newer recruits to the IS organization, however, are frustrated by Subdued's carefree attitude and feel that he became client services director because he was looking for an easy job in which to bide his time until he retired.

Subdued reports to VP of IS Sid Slicker.

Nancy Nononsenz, Vice-President of Sales and Marketing

Nancy Nononsenz, 33, is an aggressive, no-nonsense executive known for her ability to make decisions quickly and then to stick to them. She's competitive, vocal, and independent. Tutored under the New York consulting firm that helped Sleepy Valley grow into the industry leader it is today, Nononsenz has adopted many aspects of the company's style. She also takes much of the credit for Sleepy Valley's growth. She sees the sales and marketing arm of the company as its most important component. She has little patience with ideas that distract her from her marketing strategies and sales reports.

Nononsenz has a poor impression of the Sleepy Valley IS organization, which she feels botched a project for her years ago. She likes to keep her department relatively technology-free. Existing technology consists primarily of stand-alone word processing and a few PCs, all of which Nononsenz purchased without assistance from IS.

Nononsenz reports to Chief Executive Officer Jed Hilly.

Larry Likestech, Sales Director

Larry Likestech, 32, rose quickly during the company's recent boom years. College-educated, Likestech continues his education by traveling frequently and attending numerous sales conferences and seminars. He keeps abreast not only of the wine industry but of the sales field as well. He's aware of the many ways in which information technologies can be used as sales tools but has been unable to convince Nononsenz to pursue his ideas. An aggressive, polished professional, Likestech sees himself as a future VP at Sleepy Valley or another company.

Likestech reports to Vice-President of Sales Nancy Nononsenz.

Frances Fiscal, Senior Vice-President of Finance

Frances Fiscal, 38, is admittedly a numbers person. She is more comfortable with concrete data than with concepts; she's a doer, not a thinker. Her job doesn't entail the interpersonal dealings involved in the jobs of the other VPs.

Fiscal has seen her status within the company rise as the company has grown. As Sleepy Valley faces cutthroat competition from the nation's alcoholic beverage industry, the company's numbers become increasingly important. As her prominence rises, Fiscal takes her job more and more seriously. She has become concerned about errors and sloppy work. She's come to enjoy her new status and would like to see her stock rise even higher.

IS has had a role in helping Fiscal to produce the reports she needs but has never taken the lead. Fiscal has always identified her specific needs and tools and IS has simply followed through with implementation and planning.

Fiscal reports to Chief Executive Officer Jed Hilly.

Frank Hilly, Vice-President of Production

Frank Hilly, 61, is a farmer turned executive. He began his career with Sleepy Valley 48 years ago, spending his summers tending the vines. By the time he was 30, he was managing the company's entire grape-growing operations. When it comes to farming techniques, Frank Hilly is the recognized expert.

Frank Hilly had to get out of the fields a few years ago after a machinery accident. At that time, he was handed his current desk job, although he still manages to get away once a week to tour the vineyards. Frank Hilly's operation is decidedly low-tech. He tends to ignore the advice of his younger farmers, who say there are ways today to integrate technology into farming and production forecasts. They feel that Frank Hilly could better manage Sleepy Valley's vineyards, which are now spread over three counties—not to mention work crews, fertilizing, spraying and picking schedules, supply and product stocks, and expected volumes—if he had the help of modern technology. Some in the bottling end of production also feel that they could benefit from today's technology.

"Phooey," says Frank Hilly. "My father built this company with his bare hands. Besides his machines and tools, all he used was a pencil and paper. Farmers don't need computers. All they need is good tools and rain."

Frank Hilly's department is almost entirely male. A handful graduated from the County Agricultural Institute while the others have only a high school education.

Frank Hilly reports to Chief Operations Officer Bill Hilly.

Now What?

You now know the situation and the players. As Sid Slicker, can you wake up your IS organization so that it can jump start the economic comeback of Sleepy Valley Vineyards? If so, how?

This is not a theoretical exercise. Sleepy Valley is a fictional case, but there are a lot of Sleepy Valleys out there. I believe strongly that a knowledge of marketing and marketing methods will change how you look at and deal with problems such as the ones described here.

To help you in this exercise, why don't you again review the thirteen steps to developing a marketing plan listed in Chapter 12? This will give you an opportunity to practice the development of your marketing plan utilizing the thirteen-step marketing approach. You can then turn this list into a worksheet to assist you as you develop a marketing plan to rescue Sleepy Valley from its dilemma. Consider it as a project for the whole of your IS department. Then and only then compare your plan with the marketing plan, given here, that one of my seminar classes came up with in response to the thirteen points. It's not the only strategy that could be implemented, but it does cover all the bases and might just be a winner.

~∾~

Phase 1

In setting your *objectives and goals,* you want to find an area in the organization where IS could have a significant impact on the business and at the same time improve IS's image. Remember that you want to establish a *measurable* outcome. Such a measurement might be the approval of a budget, the recognition by clients of the value of IS, or the gaining of market shares.

Audience Profile. The target audience is Sleepy Valley's sales department from top to bottom. Its needs are to take sales operations into the twenty-first century without disrupting them during this highly competitive period. The department's ten-year-old systems just don't cut it any longer. The work environment is fast-paced and somewhat tense. The department is feeling severe growing pains. Nancy Nononsenz will not tolerate disruption of her department's work schedule and feels strongly that its strength is her well-chosen staff—the people, not machines. The key to selling her on new information technologies is to convince her that they are necessary to protect the market share Sleepy Valley has built up over the past ten years and to show her that the company's competitors are already using this technology. She should also be shown how the technology will help her to get the most from her talented staff. Larry Likestech, her sales director, who already uses a lap-top computer to take notes at conferences and to handle his correspondence while traveling, is likely to be an asset to the IS organization in its attempt to implement a new system.

The audience is also the entire senior level of the company, whose names, positions, and most relevant characteristics are charted in Figure 18-1. Age is included as a characteristic that is likely to have an impact on their views and understanding of IS. The company has already been identified as primarily male, conservative, and slow to accept change.

Although the head of the sales department, Nancy No-nonsenz, is skeptical of IS, some members of the IS department have a good relationship with her sales director, Larry Likestech, who seems to support the ideas of modernizing the department through technology. The sales and marketing staffs have mixed feelings about IS and technology. Those who are newer to the company, many of whom were recruited from large companies during Sleepy Valley's boom period, are aware of how helpful technology can be as a sales tool. Those who have been with the company longer are reluctant to consider technology and point to the progress the company has made without computerization. They're unfamiliar with and intimidated by new technology. The main *positive forces* for change, above and beyond the pressure of the market itself, are the support of the CEO and a progressive IS VP.

The *negative forces* against change include a bad IS image, old family ideals, the ultraconservatism of the company, the chief operations officer, a reactive finance organization, the company's small business mentality, and the plan to downsize IS. At this stage, you should apply the force field analysis shown in Figure 18-2.

Figure 18-1. Sleepy Valley Vineyards organizational chart.

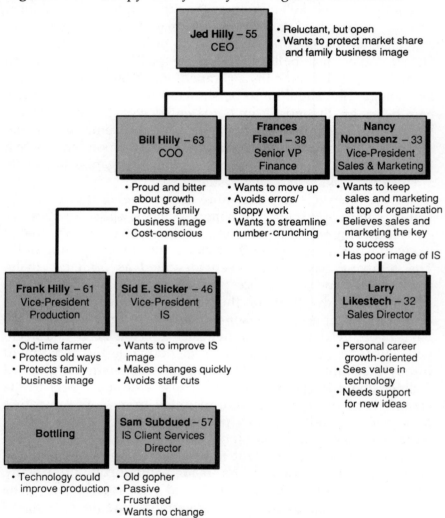

Note : Company has gone from easy growth to tough competition.

Primary Concerns and Approach. The primary concerns of IS in this scenario are Nancy Nononsenz's poor image of IS, her general resistance to technology, and her fear of any interference with current sales operations at a critical time. Additional concerns have to do with cost, timing, design,

Figure 18-2. Force field analysis applied to Sleepy Valley Vineyards.

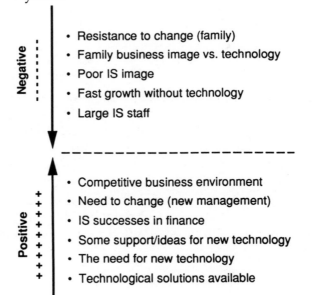

Negative
- Resistance to change (family)
- Family business image vs. technology
- Poor IS image
- Fast growth without technology
- Large IS staff

Positive
- Competitive business environment
- Need to change (new management)
- IS successes in finance
- Some support/ideas for new technology
- The need for new technology
- Technological solutions available

personnel, categorization of IS as an overhead, and IS's lack of
marketing skills.

Because the sales and marketing department is so concerned
about holding onto the market share it has just built up, the
approach of IS must be to appeal to that need. Tell sales what
systems are in place in the sales and marketing organizations of
competitors, particularly those who have an edge. Show how this
system would help Sleepy Valley, which is finally emerging as a
major player, to hold onto and enhance its market share into the
next century. Show how the system is adaptable, reputable,
flexible, and expandable. Show how it can absorb growth as well
as foster it. As a hard sell, explain how in the short term the
system will provide value to the sales organization. As a soft sell,
explain how in the long term the sales department's success can
be applied to other departments.

A good theme to introduce at this point would be "Hands
Across the Table"—the idea of IS and management jointly placing
their hands on the product and collectively charging its batteries

to obtain ever greater profits (see Figure 18-3). An alternative theme might be "One Bunch—We Grow Together"—using a bunch of grapes to stress the mutual importance of all business functions (see Figure 18-4).

Phase 2

To find partners, the IS organization should look within for the people most experienced in working with sales departments and then have them work directly with sales and marketing to get a crystal-clear picture of their needs and to fully understand their work environment. All this will ease implementation.

On the sales side, IS must try to strengthen its ties with Larry Likestech so that he can link up IS with people in his organization who are most open to new technologies. It should also work towards partnering with the senior finance VP and Young Farmers of America.

Phase 3

Your initial *marketing plan* approach might feature a morning session with Sleepy Valley sales managers Likestech and No-nonsenz for the purpose of explaining to them the benefits of a system and demonstrating how it works. Sleepy Valley players represent the extremes of "tradition vs. technology" found in typical old family-owned companies of today. Obviously those who value the traditional and reject the technological must be targeted for enlightenment.

Later you can have Sid Slicker, the IS VP, address Nancy Nononsenz separately to emphasize how important the sales department's needs are to IS and how committed IS is to the company's continued sales growth. But whatever methods you use to enlighten holdouts, just don't do it with numbers. Number-crunching, you may remember, is all that nonbelievers think IS is good for.

Graphics. I.S. must first develop a graphics capability and train its people to use graphics to their best advantage. Based on the old adage that one picture is worth a thousand words, your

Figure 18-3. "Hands Across the Table" theme.

presentations to the reactionaries should feature charts, graphs, illustrations, and even art. Visuals, even those that rely on numbers, should be presented in eye-catching color. Every item in the presentation should be entertaining as well as informative, and every attention given to the development of the "human side."

You must convince Nancy Nononsenz, for example, that the

Figure 18-4. "One Bunch" theme for Sleepy Valley Vineyards.

- ONE BUNCH -
WE GROW TOGETHER

use of technology will not undermine her own strategies and reports. IS can show her how customer lists can be developed and how direct-mail pieces can be customized; how advertising ideas can be previewed before assignment to an agency; how sales brochures can be designed; how charts and graphs can accompany the numbers, reflecting sales and/or competitive markets; and how demographics can be programmed for a better analysis of sales territories.

These same visual techniques should be used to convert Frank Hilly, the company's production VP. Especially in the production area, IS must concentrate on making numbers interesting. For example, graphs and charts showing growing, fertilizing, spraying, and picking schedules could be superimposed on U.S weather reports and demographic consumption projections, in relation to supply procurement and personnel scheduling.

The Sleepy Valley case presents a barrier to the expansion of technology mostly because of people peculiarities. People like pictures. They like to be entertained. When they see their own ideas visualized and readily available for expansion and publication, they are likely to relent, especially when the IS marketing program does not require drastic increases in cost or personnel.

The use of creative, graphic presentations may be new to a lot of people. It will require a major adjustment within the IS department. But the technology is there, and who can better employ it than the technologists? So we begin our proselytizing task by first converting ourselves to our full technological capabilities. In the process we humanize IS, perhaps the most crucial step in IS's ongoing struggle to bring the fruits of technology to the organizations it serves.

You now know the secrets of marketing. Go forth and market IS, and may the force be with you.

Appendix

Marketing Assessment of Your Organization

To find out whether your IS organization could benefit by marketing, simply respond to the following statements by checking off True or False. True answers place you among the peak-performing IS marketing professionals. False answers mean your situation is below par.

	True	False
1. We have a realistic, long-range plan for assessing and meeting our clients' needs.	___	___
2. We easily find and train excellent instructors and speakers, develop new workbook materials, and design new brochures.	___	___
3. We have attained all the volume and growth we want.	___	___
4. We know our position in the corporation, and we have established ourselves securely enough to ward off both internal and external competitors.	___	___
5. We have an ongoing system for taking the pulse of our clients so that we will know what they most want.	___	___
6. Our IS marketing communications materials (printed and nonprinted) are tops.	___	___

7. We consistently test our marketing ideas and programs against measurable criteria in an attempt to improve our position through new approaches. ___ ___

8. Our internal IS marketing brochures look different from most outside marketing materials. ___ ___

9. Our marketing materials emphasize the benefits of working with IS. ___ ___

10. We offer top-quality, exclusive features that distinguish us from other IS service centers. ___ ___

11. We regularly update our client profiles and lists. ___ ___

12. We track our clients' technology usage and technology awareness and use this information to bring improved services to our clients. ___ ___

13. We have developed a profile of our clients that lists all their important characteristics (geographic location, age, application, life cycle, size, job function, sex, education, group, resources, benefits sought, problems, client status, loyalty status, decision process, attitude, and sensitivity). ___ ___

14. We have seriously considered several marketing communications (e.g., user coordinators, external publications, management reporting, and newsletters) to make our clients aware of our value-added services. ___ ___

15. We have tested to determine how price-sensitive our prospects and clients are to our services. ___ ___

16. Our marketing communications entice new prospects, encourage repeat business, and build client loyalty. ___ ___

17. We are acutely aware of the latest and most successful approaches to marketing IS internally. ___ ___

18. We are always invited to our clients' strategic planning meetings. _____ _____

19. We know our numbers (i.e., opportunity, marketing, variable, and overhead costs; break-even points; the relationship between costs) and we use these numbers for planning our IS marketing strategy. _____ _____

20. We have a consistent and thorough system for eliciting information, as well as suggestions and evaluations, from all our clients. _____ _____

21. The decision makers in our client organizations know the details and benefits of our services. _____ _____

22. We have an IS professional development curriculum that consistently produces topnotch marketing- and client-oriented IPPs. _____ _____

23. Our services exceed client expectations and receive enthusiastic reviews. _____ _____

24. We have all the staff and resources we need for accomplishing all our important projects in the time we need to accomplish them. _____ _____

25. We have no problem justifying and getting approval for our budgets. _____ _____

Interpreting Your Score

Count up the number of statements that you checked off as *True*. Locate that number on the following chart to determine your IS marketing needs:

0–7	Marketing is unknown in your organization.
8–12	Marketing plays a minor role.
13–17	Marketing is recognized but not a force.

18–22	Marketing is taken seriously. A formal marketing plan is advised.
23–25	Marketing know-how is evident. IS is recognized as an integral business asset.

Index